Georgia Voices

# Georgia Voices

Volume Three: Poetry

EDITED BY HUGH RUPPERSBURG

The University of Georgia Press | Athens and London

© 2000 by the University of Georgia Press
Athens, Georgia 30602
All rights reserved
Designed by Kathi Morgan
Set in 10.5 on 14 Minion by G&S Typesetters, Inc.
Printed and bound by McNaughton & Gunn
The paper in this book meets the guidelines for
permanence and durability of the Committee on
Production Guidelines for Book Longevity of the
Council on Library Resources.

Printed in the United States of America

04   03   02   01   00   C   5   4   3   2   1

04   03   02   01   00   P   5   4   3   2   1

The Library of Congress has cataloged Volume 1 as follows:

Library of Congress Cataloging-in-Publication Data

Georgia voices / edited by Hugh Ruppersburg
    p.   cm.
Includes bibliographical references.
Contents: v. 1. Fiction.
1. American literature—Georgia.   2. Georgia—Literary collections.
I. Ruppersburg, Hugh M.
PS558.G4G44   1992   813.008'09758   91-36688
Volume 1. Fiction
   ISBN 0-8203-1432-3 (alk. paper)
   ISBN 0-8203-1433-1 (pbk: alk. paper)
Volume 2. Nonfiction
   ISBN 0-8203-1625-3 (alk. paper)
   ISBN 0-8203-1626-1 (pbk: alk. paper)
Volume 3. Poetry
   ISBN 0-8203-2167-2 (alk. paper)
   ISBN 0-8203-2177-X (pbk: alk. paper)

British Library Cataloging-in-Publication Data available

Contents

Preface

This is the third in a series of volumes devoted to writings by authors from the state of Georgia. The first volume presented a chronologically organized survey of selections from the state's best fiction writers, extending from Augustus Baldwin Longstreet in 1836 to Mary Hood in the 1990s. The second volume took a similar chronological approach to nonfiction in the state, beginning with Cherokee myths and legends and Oglethorpe's journals through the Civil War letters in *Children of Pride* to the oratory of Martin Luther King Jr. and the narratives of James Kilgo and Melissa Fay Greene. This third volume of *Georgia Voices* is different. Although it presents examples of the best work by Georgia's poets, for the most part it contains poetry from the last fifty years of the twentieth century. The main reason for this change is simply that much of the early poetry written by Georgians is not especially noteworthy. Even Thomas Holley Chivers, native of Washington, Georgia, and rival of Edgar Allan Poe (whom he accused of plagiarizing his work) is primarily notable as a figure of secondary importance among nineteenth-century Southern writers. The one exception from the nineteenth century who appears in the third volume is Sidney Lanier, whose poems "The Marshes of Glynn" and "Song of the Chattahoochee" make him indispensable among Georgia writers.

In choosing the poets and poems for this collection, I applied several criteria. First, poets chosen for the volume had to have spent significant periods of their lives in the state of Georgia, whether they were born here or moved here, whether they were permanent or temporary residents. Second, they had to have published at least one book of poetry with a recognized press, not including chapbooks. Poets, poetry journals, and anthologies of poetry have proliferated in recent decades. Because I could not read every poem ever published by poets with Georgia connections, I narrowed my search to poets whose work and reputations had merited the publication of at least one book of poems (although this did not guarantee inclusion). I made one exception: Phil Williams is a prolific novelist and a fine poet. Since he has edited a Georgia poetry journal, *Ataraxia,* I thought it appropriate that his work should appear. The final criterion was simply that of quality: I chose poets who have written excellent poems.

Many poets are writing in Georgia today, young and old, and their verse is often impressive and compelling. Their absence from this volume by no means indicates dismissal of their work. The predilections of any anthologist, as much as he might resist them, inevitably and perhaps insidiously manifest themselves in the kind of work to which he is attracted. Thus, although I have tried to choose in objective fashion poems that strike me as representative and meritorious, my own inclinations are undoubtedly reflected here.

Initially I wanted to include a wide selection of types of poetry in this collection: folk songs, song lyrics, street poetry, and oral verse, for example. This did not prove feasible. To include a representative sampling of these other types of poetry would have resulted in a volume that, while more inclusive, would have lacked depth. The poems included represent American and Georgia poetry in a formal and traditional sense well recognized by readers, colleges and high schools, and commercial book publishers, a kind of poetry that represents a conventional but nonetheless exciting mainstream in the poetic tradition.

I am deeply indebted to a number of individuals for their assistance with this volume. My research assistant Sandra Hughes provided help with library work and with uncovering biographical information. I am especially grateful to Kellie Borders for her invaluable help during many stages of this project. Barbara Sweetser and Barbara Crump also provided essential clerical assistance. I am grateful as well to Judith Ortiz Cofer, Stephen Corey, the late James Dickey, Anthony Grooms, and Judson Mitcham for their advice and suggestions. I thank Stanley W. Lindberg, editor of the *Georgia Review*, for his assistance and encouragement, and for the "Roots in Georgia" conference that he organized in 1985 — it helped persuade me of the value of literature produced in this state. The excellent staff of the University of Georgia Library and its rich collection of modern American literature made the preparation of this volume much easier than it could have been. The English Department of the University of Georgia provided essential research assistance and copying, as did the Franklin College of Arts and Sciences and its dean, Wyatt W. Anderson, to whom I am especially grateful. Karen Orchard, director of the University of Georgia Press, has been an unstinting supporter of the *Georgia Voices* series, and her staff has always been helpful and pleasant to work with.

To Edward Krickel, late faculty member in the English Department at the University of Georgia, I owe special tribute. From an early date he impressed on me the importance of place in literature, whether that place was the American South, New England, France, or Russia. He expressed a specific interest in these collections of Georgia writings. His fondness for Southern poetry and his belief in its value were an important source of inspiration.

I am most grateful of all to my mother, Margaret Caruthers Ruppersburg; my wife, Tricia; and my sons, Michael, Charles, and Max, for their forbearance and their love. To them, and to the people of Georgia, this anthology is dedicated.

Acknowledgments

The Press and I would like to acknowledge the poets and publishers who gave us permission to reprint material in this volume. They are:

"Psychomachia" and "Exile" by Conrad Aiken. From *Selected Poems* by Conrad Aiken. Copyright © 1961 by Conrad Aiken. Used by permission of Oxford University Press, Inc.

"A Section of the Oconee near Watkinsville," "Hymenoptera," and "New Year's Day Nap" by Coleman Barks. Reprinted by permission of the author.

"Song to Okra," "Song to Grits," and "Song to Chitlins" by Roy Blount Jr. Copyright © 1987 Roy Blount Jr. Reprinted by permission of International Creative Management, Inc.

"Time Was, She Declares," "Christmas Basket: 1943," "Burial," and "On the Fall Line" from *Time Was, She Declares* by Adrienne Bond. Reprinted by permission of Mercer University Press.

"Free Grace at Rose Hill," "Snake on the Etowah," "Shooting Rats at the Bibb County Dump," "Coasting toward Midnight at the Southeastern Fair," "Recording the Spirit Voices," and "In a U-Haul North of Damascus" from *Armored Hearts* © 1995 by David Bottoms. Reprinted by permission of Copper Canyon Press, P. O. Box 271, Port Townsend, WA 98368.

"Spaces" and "Numbers" from *Collected Poems* by Edgar Bowers. Copyright © 1997 by Edgar Bowers. Reprinted by permission of Alfred A. Knopf, Inc.

"Novas" by Van K. Brock. First published in *The Southern Review*. Reprinted by permission of the author.

"All Hallows Eve" and "Hawk" by Kathryn Stripling Byer. Reprinted by permission of the author. "The Backwoods," "For Jim on Siler's Bald," and "Thieves" from *Girl in the Midst of the Harvest* by Kathryn Stripling Byer. Reprinted by permission of Texas Tech University Press.

"The New Dolores Leather Bar," "The Chinaberry Tree," "Other Directed," and "In the land of great aunts" by Turner Cassity. Reprinted by permission of the author.

"Can You See Them?," "Mixed Drink," and "At the Warwick Hotel" by Pearl Cleage. Reprinted by permission of the author.

"Before the Storm" by Judith Ortiz Cofer. Reprinted from Martín Espada, ed., *El Coro: A Chorus of Latino and Latina Poetry* (Amherst: University of Massachusetts Press, 1997). Copyright © 1997 by Martín Espada. "Notes for My Daughter Studying Math on the Morning of a New Year" by Judith Ortiz Cofer first published in the *Kenyon Review*—New Series, Summer/Fall 1998, Vol. 20, Nos. 3/4. Reprinted by permission of the author. "First Job: The Southern Sweets Sandwich Shop and Bakery" by Judith Ortiz Cofer first published by *The Southern Review*. Reprinted by permission of the author. "Where You Need to Go" by Judith Ortiz Cofer. Reprinted by permission of the author. "The Dream of Birth" from *Reaching for the Mainland and Selected New Poems* by Judith Ortiz Cofer. © 1995 Bilingual Press/Editorial Bilingüe, Arizona State University, Tempe, AZ. Reprinted by permission of the publisher.

"Attacking the *Pietà*" by Stephen Corey. Reprinted by permission of the author.

"Sugar Cane," "After Neruda," and "The Shouters" from *Present* by Alfred Corn. Copyright © 1997 by Alfred Corn. Reprinted by permission of Counterpoint Press, a member of Perseus Books, L.L.C.

"Of Jayne Mansfield, Flannery O'Connor, My Mother & Me" and "The Distant War" from *Fort Bragg and Other Points South* by Rosemary Daniell. © 1988 by Rosemary Daniell. Reprinted by permission of Henry Holt and Company, Inc.

"The Lifeguard," "In the Mountain Tent," "Cherrylog Road," "Drinking from a Helmet," "Pursuit from Under," and "For the Last Wolverine" from *Poems 1957–1967* by James Dickey. Reprinted by permission of the University Press of New England. "Looking for the Buckhead Boys" from *The Eye-Beaters* by James Dickey. Copyright © 1970 by James Dickey. Copyright renewed 1998 by Christopher Dickey, Kevin Dickey, and Bronwen Dickey. Reprinted by permission of Theron Raines, agent.

"The Song of the Smoke," "The Song of America," and "In God's Gardens" by W. E. B. Du Bois. Reprinted by permission of David Graham Du Bois.

"Midway," "Bible Camp," and "Winter in the South" from *How the Dead Bury the Dead* by William Greenway. Reprinted by permission of the University of Akron Press.

"The Season of the Falling Face" by Walter Griffin first published in the *Sewanee Review.* Reprinted by permission of the author. "Day of the Soft Mouth" by Walter Griffin first published in the *Louisville Review.* Reprinted by permission of the author. "Fish Leaves" by Walter Griffin first published in the *Southern Review.* Reprinted by permission of the author.

"The Foreign Element" and "A Death That Dare Not Speak . . ." from *Aid and Comfort* by Greg Johnson. "The Foreign Element" was first published in *Poetry* and "A Death That Dare Not Speak . . ." was first published in the *Ontario Review.* Reprinted by permission of the author.

"Origin of the Species," "Blackberries," "First Eclogue," and "Wilderness" by Frank Manley. Reprinted by permission of the author.

"Shaving My Legs with Ockham's Razor," "Etruscan Head," "Good Friday, Driving Home," and "Snapshots: Annie Davis" by Frances Mayes. Reprinted by permission of the author.

"From My Grandmother's Diary, West Armuchee, Georgia, 1887," "Mules in New York," and "Howard Beach, Bensonhurst, Etc." by Susie Mee. Reprinted by permisison of the author.

"Notes for a Prayer in June," "Night Ride, 1965," "Somewhere in Ecclesiastes," and "Sunday" by Judson Mitcham. Reprinted by permisison of the author.

"Aunt Emma, Uncle Al: A Short History of the South," "Lines for Ben Slaughter," and "Fishing Cloud Creek, Oglethorpe County August under

Thunderheads" by Marion Montgomery. Reprinted by permission of the author.

"Three Die in Seconds," "Where Horses Once Were," and "The Interpretation of Waking Life" by Eric Nelson. Reprinted by permission of the author.

"A Child's Christmas in Georgia, 1953" by Wyatt Prunty. "Falling through the Ice," "The Lake House," and "The Depression, the War, and Gypsy Rose Lee" by Wyatt Prunty. Reprinted by permission of the author.

"Irma Lee" and "To Speak of the World As If There Were No Other" by Alane Rollings. Reprinted by permission of the author.

"The Gift of Time" and "The Alarm" from *Lanced in Light*, copyright © 1967 by Larry Rubin, reprinted by permission of Harcourt Brace & Company. "Instructions for Dying" and "Bus Terminal" by Larry Rubin. Reprinted by permission of the author.

"Charlie Walks the Night," "Three Women Named Rebecca," "Don't Send Me Off Like Some Three-Legged Dog," and "Miracle at Raven Gap" by Bettie Sellers. Reprinted by permission of the author.

"Omnipotence" from *The Palms* by Charlie Smith. Copyright © 1993 by Charlie Smith. Reprinted by permission of W. W. Norton & Company, Inc. "The Sweetness of a Peach," "Jehovah's Witness," "What Can Be United," and "Passage" by Charlie Smith. Reprinted by permission of the author.

"Water Tower," "Leaving Forever," and "Declaiming" by Ron Smith. Reprinted by permission of the author.

"An Inkling" by Leon Stokesbury. Reprinted by permission of the author.

"He Makes a House Call," "Losing a Voice in Summer," "The Truck," and "Whittling: The Last Class" by John Stone. Reprinted by permission of the author.

"Portrait in Georgia," "Georgia Dusk," and "Cotton Song" from *Cane* by Jean Toomer. Copyright 1923 by Boni & Liveright, renewed 1951 by Jean Toomer. Reprinted by permission of Liveright Publishing Corporation.

Introduction

In his recent book *The Fable of the Southern Writer*, Lewis Simpson argued that contemporary Southern writing has suffered a falling off, that contemporary writers have no memory of the Civil War, and that it remains for other writers, most specifically African American writers, to revive Southern literature sometime in the next century. Several years ago in the journal *American Literature*, literary scholar Michael Kreyling criticized the editors of a traditional history of Southern literature for taking too parochial a view of their subject and warned that the study of Southern literature might soon die out. Frank Lentricchia, in a *South Atlantic Quarterly* article on Don DeLillo, criticized Reynolds Price and Eudora Welty for being too limited by regionalism. The *Columbia Literary History of the United States* refers to regionalism as a "diminished thing." Jefferson Humphries, in his introduction to *Southern Literature and Literary Theory*, has also predicted the end of Southern literature. And a recent article in the *New Yorker* on Louisiana author James Wilcox described the difficulties this talented author has encountered in a literary marketplace where Southern writing has been significantly devalued.

The notion that literary regionalism is important is bound up in the sense that place is distinctive, and in the idea that those who inhabit a particular region, such as the South, or Georgia, must necessarily possess a sense of place. That is, they feel a sense of kinship, they feel loyal to it in some way, they feel formed by it, it is part of their identity. In a more complex way the idea of regionalism is associated with political, cultural, social, and moral beliefs identified as typical of a particular area. Conflicting positions on such issues as slavery, states' rights, agriculture, and industry fundamentally divided the South and the North as early as the seventeenth century and led ultimately to the Civil War in the nineteenth century. This view of regionalism posits that the literature of a specific region reflects these distinct values, and that it can as a result be distinguished from literature produced in other parts of the nation.

This view helped form traditional attitudes toward the literature of the American South. It is seriously flawed, especially in its assumption of regional unanimity—the notion that the people or the literature of a region will reflect the same basic characteristics, values, moral codes, and political convictions. The Southern Agrarians, authors of the 1930 cultural manifesto *I'll Take My Stand,* considered the South a distinctive region whose unique values, codes, and beliefs they wanted to celebrate and preserve. Many of the Agrarians were teachers and critics of literature who influenced several generations of Southern critics and authors. The body of opinions they generated became a kind of literary barometer that served to measure the worth of literature in the American South. Writers whose work reflected a vision of the same South promoted by the Agrarians often found a place in the textbooks they produced and the classes they taught. The best of them won recognition as great Southern writers. Those whose work did not accord with the Agrarian vision often languished in obscurity. Thus, such significant writers as Richard Wright and Zora Neale Hurston did not appear in the Southern canon for many years, nor did writers such as Lillian Smith or Frances Newman, who expressed views of the South at odds with prevailing attitudes.

Seven decades ago the notion that most or all of the people living in Georgia shared common values and experience might have been valid, for in 1930 only 10 percent of the people living in Georgia were from outside the state. Today over 35 percent of the people living in Georgia were born outside the state, and if we add the people whose parents were born somewhere else, the number grows. In Atlanta, a city that has taken on an increasingly international character, the number climbs even higher. Transportation systems that allow people to travel from one state to another easily and cheaply have contributed to an economy that does not depend on individuals living in one place for their entire lives—indeed, it depends on just the opposite. Advances in communication and the growth of mass media have also diminished the importance of regionalism. Television, movies, the national media, friends and teachers from other states and countries—all these have contributed to the formation of personal values that are not derived from regional loyalties. What this means is that many if not most of the people in the state do not hold many values and experiences in common. The forces that shape character, personal values, beliefs, moral codes, and so on no longer originate primarily in the region of one's birth. The influences that helped mold the Southernness of Margaret Mitchell or William Faulkner or Flannery O'Connor have changed vastly or even disappeared entirely, and Southerners today are the product of numerous complexly interwoven forces from inside and outside the region. They are no longer Southern in the traditional sense. Nor, for the most part, are many of the contemporary Georgia poets whose works are collected in these pages.

In his introduction to *Songs and Poems of the South* (1857), the nineteenth-century Georgia poet Thomas Holley Chivers wrote that "the poetry of a country should be a faithful expression of its physical and moral characteristics." Poetry in contemporary Georgia continues to reflect the place and times of its origins. Poets in general are observant of their surroundings, of the family, the community, the historical period, and the natural environment in which they live. It is not surprising, therefore, that Georgia poets would write about their world, and that we should encounter that world as we read their poems. Because they live in and to varying extents write about the state, and because we assume that we will find in their work attitudes and concerns representative of their region, we describe them as Southern, as Georgian. Yet "place and times" no longer limit us to specific geographical boundaries as they once did: in the twentieth century, "place and times" may simply refer to the world at large, to a global society on the cusp of the millennium. Automobiles, airplanes, telephones, television, and the Internet have exploded the concept of place to include, potentially, the entire world, and the times may reflect the prevailing values and opinions of a region more vast than one part of the southeastern United States. In that sense the Persian Gulf War, the bombing of the Federal Office Building in Oklahoma City, and the AIDS epidemic are as much a part of the "times" for poets in Georgia as are incidents and people closer to home. Thus it is possible for such a poet as Turner Cassity, of Atlanta, to write poems about such traditional Southern icons as "The Chinaberry Tree" and "great aunts" ("In the land of great aunts") and also to describe, in "The New Dolores Leather Bar"—a poem that offers what is perhaps the greatest contrast and paradox of any in this volume—how farmers and mechanics seek companionship and satisfaction in drag bars at night.

To put this another way: Georgia poets who write about their state do so because it happens to be where they live and because the situations, people, and events it confronts them with are what they know most directly. Most of them do not write about their state because they love it or because they wish to pay homage to it, but because it is inescapably part of their experience. At the same time, the boundaries of the world that Georgia poets write about stretch far beyond the borders of the state. The subjects they write about are not, for the most part, regional. They are subjects that affect all of us as Americans, or that because of their universal impact (death, love, family) affect all of us as members of the human race.

In this sense Georgia poets are as representative of the nation as they are of the state. Most of the traits in Georgia poetry that we might tentatively identify as regional would ultimately be found among poets in other parts of the United States and the world. It is more appropriate to think of Georgia poets as American poets, or as poets of the English language, than it is to think of them as merely Southern poets, as poets of Georgia.

Not every poet in Georgia necessarily has chosen to be a "Georgia" poet. Born in Savannah of parents from New England, Conrad Aiken spent most of his adult life outside Georgia, and most of his poetry does not concern the state. One might argue that his Southern upbringing nonetheless informed his poetry, though such arguments are meaningless without tangible evidence. Some of his poems employ the rhetoric of Southern forms: "Blues for Ruby Matrix," for instance, begins as the lyric for a blues song. Other poems show a sensitivity to landscape, a sense that the land plays a role in defining individual identity. And in a few fiction and nonfiction pieces Aiken does write about the place of his birth. For the most part, however, he proves an exception who does not contribute to the traditional definitions of Georgia poetry. One might say much the same of Edgar Bowers, Alfred Corn, or even Wyatt Prunty. Yet by not conforming to traditional definitions of regional poetry, these poets help forge a more meaningful understanding of what poetry in this state can be.

Nonetheless, when we consider poets from Georgia as a group, we naturally want to try to characterize and categorize them, to seek out common threads, to find a sense of cultural community and kinship, of political solidarity. We soon discover that this is a difficult task. Consistent with contemporary American poetry in general, for instance, much recent Georgia poetry is not strongly political. It tends to address such matters as personal relationships, family, and nature. In so doing, it may still reflect political attitudes (the muted feminism of Alane Rollings, for instance, or Jean Toomer's celebration of African American farm workers in middle Georgia). A few poets more openly and forcefully engage political issues: Sidney Lanier's poems "Corn" and "Thar's More in the Man Than Thar Is in the Land" celebrate the importance of agriculture to the Southern economy and, when they were published at the end of the nineteenth century, contributed to the debate between advocates of the New South and advocates of the Agrarian South. More recently, both Alice Walker and Pearl Cleage have written about issues of race and of womanhood. Rosemary Daniell, in prose and verse, undertakes a severe examination of the position of women in the modern South. Greg Johnson's poems about AIDS are political in the sense that they call attention to a national health crisis, though at the same time they more directly concern such fundamental human issues as grief and death, the loss of friends. In his powerful long poem "A Christmas Murder," Alfred Corn effectively weaves into a single strand the long tradition of racist violence with the persecution of homosexuals. Even Byron Herbert Reece, rustic bard of the North Georgia mountains, expresses political attitudes. In his poem "Roads," for instance, he observes the cars passing back and forth on highways near his city door and then passes judgment: "My heart is native to the sky / Where hills that are its only wall / Stand up to judge its boundaries by." Tall skyscrapers and hard concrete "bruise the country heel / My heart's contracted to a stone":

> Therefore, whatever roads repair
> To cities on the plain, my own
> Lead upward to the peaks; and there
> I feel, pushing my ribs apart,
> The wide sky entering my heart.

This is a clearly agrarian poem: conservative, anti-industrial, and anti-urban in its hostility to the hurly-burly city and its preference for the open air of the mountains. Moreover, the poem is a clear declaration of allegiance to the mountains, to the countryside, to everything that is not the city—in the mountains, Reece is saying, he finds his identity, his inspiration, his life's blood. It is in fact difficult to find many Southern poems that have much to say about city life, though Pearl Cleage, in "Can You See Them?," "Mixed Drink," and "At the Warwick Hotel," is a refreshing exception.

Three relatively common subjects or themes tend to link Georgia poets to each other and to their state. These are nature and the natural world, family, and tradition or heritage. A fourth broad theme links Georgia poets to the world at large. It can best be characterized with an expression that William Faulkner used in his 1950 Nobel Prize acceptance speech: "old verities and truths of the heart, the universal truths lacking which any story is ephemeral and doomed—love and honor and pity and pride and compassion and sacrifice." These verities and "truths of the heart" have been the subject of poetry—of all great literature—since the first poems were written.

North Carolina poet and novelist Fred Chappell recently observed that what sets much Southern poetry apart is its "vision of nature." Nature was a central subject for Georgia's first great poet, Sidney Lanier. He was a talented artist of national prominence in his day, both as a musician and as a writer. His total poetic output fills a volume of slightly more than one hundred pages. (His critical and musical writings are more extensive.) Not often anthologized today, he nonetheless wrote several poems—especially "The Marshes of Glynn" and "Song of the Chattahoochee"—that continue to live. The beauty in these poems comes from the natural music of Lanier's language, and from his ability to evoke landscape and its emotional impact on the observer. In "Song of the Chattahoochee," he playfully manipulates meter, line length, and geographical place names in a poem that both imitates the sound of the rippling waters of the upper Chattahoochee and summons up the geography of the entire state:

> Out of the hills of Habersham,
>   Down the valleys of Hall,
> I hurry amain to reach the plain,
> Run the rapid and leap the fall.

"The Marshes of Glynn" is a more serious and introspective study of coastal landscape and its effect on human consciousness, on what Lanier would call the soul. It is one of the finest poems of the nineteenth century. Written in the tradition of Walt Whitman and the transcendental writers Emerson and Thoreau, "The Marshes of Glynn" impressionistically describes the tidal marshes near Brunswick as the tide changes and night falls.

James Dickey's treatment of nature, which in some sense harkens back to Whitman and Lanier, is at the same time considerably different. Fred Chappell has observed that "the Southern poet often sees nature as a dangerous and inimical force, a field of contest. . . . This outlook seems to have become a central one only after James Dickey gained so much power from it in his work." Dickey's influence over modern Southern poetry has been considerable. He often argued against the notion that a poet wrote out of any tradition at all, disagreeing sharply with T. S. Eliot's notion, expressed in "Tradition and the Individual Talent," that the poet is bound by or has a responsibility to traditions forged by earlier writers. In his life and his writing Dickey was a fierce individualist. He matured in the 1950s, when the American confessional poets, most notably Robert Lowell, were approaching their primes, and in much of his poetry he himself plays the confessional role, though usually in a sense that is more retrospective (describing past experiences and friendships) than intensely self-scrutinizing. Dickey projects the self he wishes to confess onto the landscape and the people around him, into the natural world, even onto the stars, as he attempts to do in his long poem *The Zodiac* (1976). The result can be bombastic and long-winded, or dramatically visionary (as his best poetry is, and there is a lot of it).

Nature is an element to which Dickey feels intensely related. It energizes and sustains him, threatens and destroys him, and he feels compelled to contend against it. In many ways his 1970 novel *Deliverance* embodies this paradoxical attraction in its tale of four men from Atlanta whose weekend canoe trip on a mountain river becomes a desperate struggle for survival. Many of his poems also explore this contradiction. In "Springer Mountain" a hunter drops the bow and arrow with which he is hunting and runs naked after a deer in the cold mountain air. In his powerful long poem "Falling" a stewardess who has fallen from an airplane seeks to dominate the air, to control nature and her place in it, before she strikes the inevitable ground. In the face of her annihilation, she feels for the first time what it truly means to be. In "Mayday Sermon," another long poem, a woman preacher evokes the powerful reproductive and sexual impulses of nature in her sermon to a congregation of women in Gilmer County. Dickey's well-known "Cherry-log Road" describes how the coupling of two lovers in an old car brings an auto junkyard to life:

So the blacksnake, stiff
With inaction, curved back
Into life, and hunted the mouse

With deadly overexcitement,
The beetles reclaimed their field
As we clung, glued together,
With the hooks of the seat springs
Working through to catch us red-handed

The poem "Pursuit from Under" presents the image that may best summarize Dickey's attitude toward nature: walking through an open field, he imagines that he hears the barking of seals and then thinks of the Eskimos, pursued from beneath the polar ice by killer whales that remain unseen until they break through the ice to devour their prey. For Dickey, the individual lives always with the knowledge of his own mortality, under the threat of a deceptively benign Nature that can suddenly turn malignant and murderous.

Dickey's death in 1997 prompted readers to reassess his achievement, both as a novelist and as a poet. A 1998 memoir by his son Christopher has presented a fresh view of this troubled, complicated, and extremely talented man. There can be little doubt that his best work will endure, and that he will be remembered as one of the greatest Georgia poets of the twentieth century—some would argue one of the finest American poets. His sway over writers who followed him has been considerable: David Bottoms has written very much under his influence, managing at the same time to develop an original and vital style that on occasion addresses the texture of contemporary Southern life more directly than did Dickey. Bottoms's poems "Shooting Rats at the Bibb County Dump" and "In a U-Haul North of Damascus" are among the finest Southern poems written in the last two decades of the century, and in such poems as "Snake on the Etowah" and "In a Pasture under a Cradled Moon" he demonstrates a sensitive and perceptive awareness of the natural world. Coleman Barks, Charlie Smith, Alane Rollings, and Stephen Corey are other poets who have developed distinctive voices yet who work in one way or the other within the tradition that Dickey's work helped shape and nurture.

Heritage is another common theme for Georgia poets—not in the old sense of reverence for ancestors that is also reverence for a vanquished order, but instead in the sense simply of reverence for those who came before. James Dickey (in "The Firebombing" and "The Helmet") and Edgar Bowers have written powerfully in this vein on the subject of World War II.

Kathryn Stripling Byer, who has taken the Appalachian mountains as her own landscape, delves deeply into her own sense of a personal heritage that one senses she regards as part of a regional and national heritage as well. In her poems she seems intensely aware of her own connections with fore-bears, whether they are hers by blood kinship or simply because they are ancestors in a more general sense—those who settled and cultivated the land, opened the wilderness, prepared for the generations to follow. Byer suggests as much in her spooky poem "All Hallows Eve," in which she imagines the spirits of three unknown people buried in graves up the hill-side from where she lives. She feels haunted by their spirits, which seem to resent her for the fact that she still lives:

No wonder they go away
always complaining how little the living
have learned, on our knees
every night asking God for a clean heart,
a pure spirit. Spirit? They kick
up the leaves round the silent house.
What good is spirit without hands for walnut
to stain, without ears for the river
to fill up with promises?

The very fact that Byer has taken the Appalachians as her chosen setting suggests a commitment to, and a concern with preserving, the tradition and heritage of the region. One may reach the same conclusion about Bettie Sellers and her mentor, Byron Herbert Reece, whose love of the North Georgia mountains represents a devotion to the heritage of that region that he sometimes reflects on in his poetry, especially in "Mountain Fiddler," where he imagines himself as a musician whose fiddling causes the dead to dance.

Alice Walker likewise expresses a strong commitment to heritage. This is the main theme of her story "Everyday Use," and in such essays as "In Search of Our Mothers' Gardens" and "In Homage to Flannery O'Con-nor" she explores the conflicting and complex meanings of this word. On the one hand she regards heritage as something to be revered; on the other it is a record of oppression. She specifically considers this aspect of heri-tage in her poem "Eagle Rock," which describes the large eagle, built out of small stones, left by the Cherokee Indians near Eatonton, Georgia. The white tourists, "Young Future Farmers," who come to gaze upon the eagle

> . . . do not know the rock
> They love
> *Lives* and is bound
> To bide its time
> To wrap its stony wings
> Around
> The innocent eager 4-H Club.

Jean Toomer explores a similar heritage in poems he included in his novel *Cane*. In "Song of the Son," for instance, he muses on the disappearance of the heritage of slavery times and is gratified that by plucking the "plum" saved for him he has the opportunity to preserve it in his writings:

> O Negro slaves, dark purple ripened plums,
> Squeezed, and bursting in the pine-wood air,
> Passing before they stripped the old tree bare
> One plum was saved for me, one seed becomes
>
> An everlasting song, a singing tree,
> Caroling softly souls of slavery,
> What they were, and what they are to me,
> Caroling softly souls of slavery.

James Dickey, in "In the Slave Quarters," considers the same heritage from the perspective of a modern white Southerner aware of the history of oppression signified in the decayed ruins of houses where slaves once lived.

As far away as they have moved from the Old South and the Civil War, a heritage that for earlier writers was too powerful to ignore, modern Georgia poets still occasionally feel its pull. In "Fog on Kennesaw" David Bottoms describes camping on the slopes of the mountain, remembers the battle that occurred there, and notes that "nothing has changed here but the century." In "Wilderness" Frank Manley describes the experiences of a man named Abner Small in the Battle of the Wilderness. Manley methodically catalogs Small's every sensation as, after he is wounded by a bursting artillery shell, he watches the flames of the burning forest approach:

As the flames licked the tips of his eyes
And the glowing coals touched his lips
He heard a voice from the burning bush
Like the sound of his breath
Inward and outward
Saying forever
I am who am
I am who am

Death in battle is Small's fate. Manley compares the fire in the forest to the Old Testament burning bush, in which God announces his presence. He portrays Small's death not as heroic but simply as an almost random event, unrelated to anything Small himself has said or done. It is a historical event in that sense, and Small is one of the thousands who in that battle became the necessary victims of history. Yet it is a personal event as well, the moment when he is called to account for his life and to meet his maker.

Phil Williams, in "The Confederate Cemetery in Madison, Georgia," is also interested in the Civil War, but he views it as an event from a past so distant that he can identify the man buried beneath a gravestone only by his first name. What Williams emphasizes, as he addresses the grave of one man in particular, is that the past is unrecoverable:

I do not believe in the resurrection
of your body, Edward. The shade
of water oaks, the sound of clear wind
Will hold you down. Your fellows
have no names, only cool marble
slabs and
the single word, unknown.

Sometimes, however, the past does assert itself, even in a comical way, as Susie Mee demonstrates in "Mules in New York," where she imagines that she sees mules "meandering down Fifth Avenue." The poem expresses her frustration over not being able to free herself of memories of her other life, "that other dream" with its mules "munching grass / beside a dirt road in Georgia."

Another important theme, one related to the idea of heritage, is that of family. During the last half of the twentieth century, American poetry has become increasingly personal. From the beginning, domestic poetry by such writers as Anne Bradstreet and Emily Dickinson focused on the inner lives of the poets and their personal experiences. In recent decades this emphasis has been especially pronounced. Poets in Georgia have been no exception. Concern with parents, wives or husbands, and children is a central preoccupation. Poets frequently explore their kinship with parents, as Judith Cofer does with her mother in her poem "The Dream of Birth," and as Susie Mee does with her grandmother in "From My Grandmother's Diary, West Armuchee, Georgia, 1887." Coleman Barks, in "New Year's Day Nap," writes movingly of his feelings as he is forced to acknowledge his son's growth toward maturity. As he watches his oldest son asleep on a sofa in front of the television on New Year's Day, he tries to link the moment of his son's conception to the present day. Barks knows he has lost his son, and he grieves. What makes this poem particularly poignant is his use of shake notes to represent the hymn that works in a kind of counterpoint throughout the poem. (When Barks reads the poem aloud, he sings the hymn, an effect difficult to duplicate on paper.)

Coming to terms with one's parents seems an especially significant way of grappling with fundamental issues of personal identity. In his poem "Sunday" Judson Mitcham explores the conflicting feelings of guilt, love, and grief he feels over his father's death, and in doing so traces his own slow progress toward adulthood. This theme in some sense has been central for the poet and novelist Charlie Smith, who in his recent collection of poems *Before and After* examines with emotional and psychological candor his attitudes toward his family and the legacy they have left him, which he explores at length in such poems as "The Sweetness of a Peach," "Talking among Ourselves," and "What Can Be United." Many poets run the risk of sentimentality when they write about family. For Smith, the opposite may be true: he is drawn by the temptation to uncover Gothic horror in the family experience. One suspects that writing about his family is a catharsis for him, a summoning up of strength to absorb and to live with their legacy. Leon Stokesbury, in his humorous and poignant "An Inkling," takes an approach to this subject that is more common among Southern and Georgia poets: he describes the first meeting of his parents with poignant humor and irony. His mother's conscious decision to allow herself to love his father has a consequence suggested in the poem's very title: "An

Inkling"—in the sense of presentiment, omen, premonition. The future Stokesbury is the inkling to which the title refers.

For David Bottoms, the failure of marriage provides the subject of one of his most powerful poems, "In a U-Haul North of Damascus." One senses in this poem the influence of James Dickey, yet struggling successfully against it is Bottoms's own anguished voice and his effort to find some hope of personal redemption in the ruins of divorce. Few poets have more successfully described the emotional devastation of divorce. The speaker in the poem feels pain over his own responsibility for the collapse of his marriage:

> Lord, what are the sins
> I have tried to leave behind me? The bad checks,
> the workless days, the Scotch bottles thrown across the fence
> and into the woods, the cruelty of silence,
> the cruelty of lies, the jealousy,
> the indifference?

The poem asks whether there is any possibility of recovery from this personal disaster. Although the speaker sees no glimmer of hope, he wonders whether, like Paul on the road to Damascus, he will "be moved to fall / toward grace."

Even those poets who identify closely with their region, poets such as Lanier or Marion Montgomery or Reece, also express a larger meditative concern with the "old verities and truths of the heart." Adrienne Bond is a fine example of a poet who melds regional settings and situations with meditations on fundamental philosophical issues. In "Time Was, She Declares" she uses modern cosmological theories about the creation and the end of the universe to engage in a whimsical meditation on time and change, on our normal inclination to want to recover the past, and the horror we should feel if we were really able to do so:

> a point in time will come, taut
> between bang and crunch, all silvery quiver
> and in perfect tune, when reach
> will momentarily equal grab,
> and we will see the things we thought we'd lost
> all pause, turn, and come avalanching

back—coins, lovers, kites and luggage,
teeth and keys and jobs,
umbrellas and the dead.

Bond centers on the difficulty of making sense of the present-time physical world in the face of scientific theories and discoveries. What physicists predict about the distant future may in fact one distant day come to pass, but what gives meaning to our brief and limited span on the earth are the things we know and trust, things that pass away never to return. Bond examines the painful facts of time, age, and racial division in her poem "Christmas Basket: 1943," in which she describes from a little girl's viewpoint a meeting between her grandmother and an old black woman who had once been her playmate. The little girl cannot understand why the black woman showed no pleasure in the reunion with her old friend, and the grandmother sharply answers her, "Tell me one reason why she should," a boldly ambiguous pronouncement that invites the reader to wonder over its meaning. Was there more joy or pain in this reunion that confronts both women with the awareness of time and impending death?

In his ambitious long poem "Attacking the *Pietà*," Stephen Corey considers the power of art to inspire vastly different reactions in different people, and the inexplicable nature of human motives. Focusing on the defacement in 1972 of Michelangelo's *Pietà* by a man named Laslo Toth, he contrasts the ambitions of the Renaissance artist to create perfection with the generations that followed him and remade his work in various versions of their own image: Toth sees Michelangelo's work as an insult to his parents and their love for him. While he remembers his own mother's kind love, in the face of the Virgin he sees something cold and different:

> That face so at ease, so glib,
> bowed as if thinking of a story
> She'd heard, and trying to be sad.
> Never hungry in Her life, never alone.
> I went for the eyes. You've seen them?
> Up close? Beneath those lids—nothing!

For the artisans who seek to restore the damaged statue, for the security guards who protect it at a world's fair, for the priests who modify it to match their own images of sacredness, and for Corey himself—who thinks

he sees in the *Pietà* the paragon of art ("her body of art, irreplaceable")—
to each of these the statue offers different meanings. For Lurleen Wallace,
whose husband was wounded and paralyzed for life by a would-be assassin
on the same day as the statue's defacement, the event epitomizes life's un-
fairness and prompts her decision to run for governor. The statue, in its
damaged perfection, takes on its own power and becomes for Corey a sym-
bol of the past, of tradition, of the incomprehensible coincidences that gov-
ern human motives and human events. Ultimately, Corey discovers in his
father's indifference to the defacement proof of the distance between them
and of his failure to understand his father, and of the weight of the past:

> My loss was not the indifference
> but the fragile void of its causes,
> the way a life we love can be steered,
> beyond our control, beyond us.

His father, in effect, is not the man Corey would have him be—he is an-
other being, a product of the "fragile void," of causes beyond his son's
control or comprehension. "We wear the past," says Corey, "like leaded
boots / on astronauts who walk the moon—/ the heavy exertion of every
step / our only chance to keep from drifting off." The past, epitomized in
the damaged and revered *Pietà*, holds different meanings for all of us. Some
of us it inspires; others it enslaves. It is a burden that may have little relation
to the motives of the artist who created it.

Assessing modern poetry in the American South, Mark Royden Winchell
has suggested that "there are perhaps three senses in which a poet can be
regarded as Southern: if he is from the South; if he writes about the South;
and if his work is informed by some sense of the region's internal contra-
dictions" (*HSL*, 318). Winchell believes that Southernness means a homo-
geneous set of attitudes and values. I would modify his first criterion to
read "if he is from or lives in the South" because Southern culture is not
homogeneous. Statistically, certain attitudes may be more common in the
South than in other parts of the world. However, the South, and especially
Georgia, has always been a place where disagreement, diversity of opin-
ion, and good-natured (occasionally not so good-natured) contentiousness
have been common. One has only to consider conflicting attitudes toward
secession expressed in the Atlanta press in the late 1850s to confirm this

observation. It was quite possible in the prewar South to be opposed to slavery or secession and to live a comfortable and happy life. (Of course, it was better not to express these attitudes openly, but the point is that they were held by people who thought of themselves as loyal Southerners.) In the twentieth century, it is quite possible for someone who has moved here from outside the region to be a "Southern" writer simply because he or she lives here and writes about the South as he or she experiences it. What the South means for such a person may be quite different from what it means for others. Moreover, such a person may perceive Southern life in a way that enables him or her to offer startling and valuable insights. Regardless of regional loyalties or disloyalties, Southerners also care about the same issues that concern people throughout the world, and they write about these issues as a result—not because they are Southern, but because they are human.

Judith Ortiz Cofer in many ways represents a new direction for contemporary Georgia. A native-born Puerto Rican who has lived most of her life in Georgia, Cofer has written almost exclusively about her Puerto Rican upbringing and her experience as an immigrant to America. This is the subject of her novel *The Line of the Sun* and of her stories in *An Island Like You: Stories of the Barrio*. In her poems "Before the Storm" and "Dream of Birth," for example, she explores her relationship with her mother (who returned to Puerto Rico following her husband's death) and to Puerto Rico itself. In "Before the Storm" she helps her mother sort through family mementoes, choosing which ones to save in the event that a hurricane bearing down on the island should sweep the house away:

> I am strangely excited.
> Knowing that I am as ready as I will ever be,
> should I have another fifty years to go,
> to go with my mother
> towards higher ground. And when we come home, if
> we come home, if there's a home where we believe
> we left one, it will all be different.

Cofer's concern here is with the potential loss of memories, which help her define and buttress her identity. The hurricane is the storm of time and of the decisions and events that come with time, including immigration to a new land. Each time Cofer returns to the home of her mother she finds it a different place from the one she encountered in her last visit, her perceptions of it increasingly influenced by her experiences on the American mainland.

Much of Cofer's work explores transcultural experiences that have informed her life as a Southerner and a Georgian. She describes her poem "First Job: The Southern Sweets Sandwich Shop and Bakery" as her first "Southern" poem. By this she apparently means that it is her first conscious attempt to write about a Southern subject with recognizably Southern characters. She is also alluding to certain Southern stereotypes that she exploits in order to see through to the reality of the people behind them. Cofer's concern with clashing cultures is a theme in this Southern poem, which contrasts her experience as the daughter of Puerto Rican parents to that of the Southern-born Lillie Mae, a waitress in the bakery:

> I'm fifteen, living my first year
> in the strange country called Georgia.
> Lillie Mae hired me for my long black hair
> she couldn't wait to braid, and for my gift
> of tongues, which she witnessed as I turned
> my mother's desire for a sugar bubble
> she called a *merengue* into something nearly equal
> behind the glass wall.

The poem is Southern in its use of setting and dialect, in the characters of Mr. Raymond and Lillie Mae, and in the candy shop itself. It is cross-cultural in its contrasting of the Southern and Latino cultures, embodied in the double entendre in the phrase "gift of tongues." Of course Cofer does not meet the requirements set forth by Winchell for a Southern writer—she is a Catholic Latina writer to whom English is a second language, for whom the South, at least initially, was a foreign land. Yet in significant ways her poem, which grows out of the changing nature of the state's population in the last twenty years, suggests a new direction for Georgia writing in the years to come.

Georgia poetry remains a diverse combination of the old and the new, of tradition and innovation. It reflects many of the themes that have proven fundamental to Georgia writers from the beginning—themes of family, community, personal integrity, the natural world—as well as concerns that we identify closely with life in the postmodern era: AIDS, war, divorce, disconnectedness. Despite the common themes and concerns that bind Georgia poets together, other concerns divide and distinguish them. As the nature of the modern South continues to change, so too does the literature it produces. While it does not seem likely that literature from the state of Georgia will cease to be distinctive anytime soon, it is clear that by the end of the new century it will have changed more fundamentally than any of us at the end of the old century could have possibly imagined.

REFERENCES

Chappell, Fred. "'Not as a Leaf': Southern Poetry and the Innovation of Tradition." *Georgia Review* 51 (Fall 1997), 477–89.

Elliott, Emory, ed. *The Columbia Literary History of the United States.* New York: Columbia UP, 1988.

Humphries, Jefferson. *Southern Literature and Literary Theory.* Athens: University of Georgia Press, 1990.

Kreyling, Michael J. "Southern Literature: Consensus and Dissensus." *American Literature* 60 (March 1988), 83–95.

Lentricchia, Frank. "The American Writer as Bad Citizen: Introducing Don DeLillo." *South Atlantic Quarterly* 89 (1990), 239–44.

Simpson, Louis J. *The Fable of the Southern Writer.* Baton Rouge: Louisiana State University Press, 1994.

Stewart, James B. "Moby Dick in Manhattan." *New Yorker* 70 (June 27, 1994), 46–66.

Winchell, Mark Royden. "The New Poetry." In *The History of Southern Literature,* ed. Louis D. Rubin. Baton Rouge: Louisiana State University Press, 1985. Pp. 314–18.

Georgia Voices

Conrad Aiken

Psychomachia

I

Tent-caterpillars, as you see, (he said)
Have nested in these cherry-trees, and stripped
All sound of leaves from them. You see their webs
Like broken harp-strings, of a fairy kind,
Shine in the moonlight.

And then I to him:

But is this why, when all the houses sleep,
You meet me here,—to tell me only this,
That caterpillars weave their webs in trees?
This road I know. I have walked many times
These sandy ruts. I know these starveling trees,
Their gestures of stiff agony in winter,
And the sharp conscious pain that gnaws them now.
But there is mystery, a message learned,
A word flung down from nowhere, caught by you,
And hither brought for me. How shines that word,
From what star comes it? . . . This is what I seek.

And he in answer: Can you hear the blood
Cry out like jangled bells from all these twigs;
Or feel the ghosts of blossom touch your face?
Walk you amid these trees as one who walks
Upon a field where lie the newly slain
And those who darkly die? And hear you crying?
Flesh here is torn from flesh. The tongue's plucked out.
What speech then would you have, where speech is tongueless,
And nothing, nothing, but a welling up of pain?

I answered; You may say these smitten trees,
Being leafless, have no tongues and cannot speak.
How comforts that my question? . . . You have come,
I know, as you come always, with a meaning.
What, then, is in your darkness of hurt trees;
What bird, sequestered in that wilderness
Of inarticulate pain, wrong ill-endured,
And death not understood, but bides his time
To sing a piercing phrase? Why sings he not?
I am familiar, long, with pain and death,
Endure as all do, lift dumb eyes to question
Uncomprehended wounds; I have my forest
Of injured trees, whose bare twigs show the moon
Their shameful floating webs; and I have walked,
As now we walk, to listen there to bells
Of pain, bubbles of blood, and ached to feel
The ghosts of blossom pass. But is there not
The mystery, the fugitive shape that sings
A sudden beauty there that comes like peace?

You know this road, he said, and how it leads
Beyond starved trees to bare grey poverty grass;
Then lies the marsh beyond, and then the beach,
With dry curled waves of sea-weed, and the sea.
There, in the fog, you hear the row-locks thump,
And there you see the fisherman come in
From insubstantial nothing to a shore
As dim and insubstantial. He is old,
His boat is old and grey, the oars are worn.
You know this,—you have seen this?

                     And then I:
I know, have seen this, and have felt the shore
As dim and thin as mist; and I have wondered
That it upheld me, did not let me fall
Through nothing into nothing . . . And the oars,

Worn down like human nerves against the world;
And the worn road that leads to sleeping houses
And weeping trees. But is this all you say?
For there is mystery, a word you have
That shines within your mind. Now speak that word.

And he in answer: So you have the landscape
With all its nerves and voices. It is yours.
Do with it what you will. But never try
To go away from it, for that is death.
Dwell in it, know its houses, and cursed trees,
And call it sorrow. Is this not enough?
Love you not shameful webs? It is enough.
There is no need for bird, or sudden peace.

II
The plain no herbage had, but all was bare
And swollen livid sand in ridges heaped;
And in the sharp cold light that filled the east
Beneath one cloud that was a bird with wings
I saw a figure shape itself, as whirling
It took up sand and moved across the sand.
A man it was, and here and there he ran
Beating his arms, now falling, rising now,
Struggling, for so it seemed, against the air.
But, as I watched, the cloud that was a bird
Lifted its wings; and the white light intense
Poured down upon him. Then I saw him, naked,
Amid that waste, at war with a strange beast
Or monster, many-armed and ever-changing;
That now was like an octopus of air,
Now like a spider with a woman's hair
And woman's hands, and now was like a vine
That wrapped him round with leaves and sudden flowers,
And now was like a huge white thistledown
Floating; and with this changing shape he fought

Furious and exhausted, till at length
I saw him fall upon it in the sand
And strangle it. Its tentacles of leaves
Fell weakly downward from his back, its flowers
Turned black. And then, as he had whirled at first,
So whirled he now again, and with his feet
Drew out the sand, and made a pit, and flung
The scorpion-woman-vine therein, and heaped
The sand above.

         And then I heard him sing
And saw him dance; and all that swollen plain
Where no herb grew, became a paradise
Of flowers, and smoking grass, and blowing trees
That shook out birds and song of birds. And he
In power and beauty shining like a demon
Danced there, until that cloud that was a bird
Let fall its wings and darkened him, and hid
The shining fields. But still for long I heard
His voice, and bird-song bells about him chiming,
And knew him dancing there above that grave.

III
Said he: Thus draw your secret sorrow forth,
Whether it wear a woman's face or not;
Walk there at dusk beside that grove of trees,
And sing, and she will come. For while she haunts
Your shameful wood with all its webs and wounds
And darkly broods and works her mischief there,
No peace you'll have, but snares, and poisonous flowers
And trees in lamentation. Call her out
As memory cries the white ghost from the tomb.
Play the sharp lyric flute, for that she loves,
With topaz phrases for her vanity.

And I in answer: She is dear to me,
Dearer that in my mind she makes a dark
Of woods and rocks and thorns and venomous flowers.
What matter that I seldom see her face,
Or have her beauty never? She is there,
It is her voice I hear in cries of trees.
This may be misery, but it is blest.

Then he: And when you have her, strongly take
Her protean fiery body and lithe arms
And wailing mouth and growing vines of hair
And leaves that turn to hands, and bear her forth
Into that landscape that is rightly yours
And dig a grave for her, and thrust her in
All writhing, and so cover her with earth.
Then will the two, as should be, fuse in one.

The landscape, that was dead, will straightway shine
And sing and flower about you, trees will grow
Where desert was, water will flash from dust,
And rocks grow out in leaves. And you, this grief
Torn from your heart and planted in your world,
Will know yourself at peace.

                        But will it be,—
I asked,—as bright a joy to see that landscape
Put on diffused her wonder, sing her name,
Burn with the vital secret of her body
There locked in earth like fire, as now to have
Her single beauty fugitive in my mind?
If she is lost, will flowering rocks give peace?

And he in answer: So you have the landscape
With all her nerves and voices . . . She is yours.

Exile

These hills are sandy. Trees are dwarfed here. Crows
Caw dismally in skies of an arid brilliance,
Complain in dusty pine-trees. Yellow daybreak
Lights on the long brown slopes a frost-like dew,
Dew as heavy as rain; the rabbit tracks
Show sharply in it, as they might in snow.
But it's soon gone in the sun—what good does it do?
The houses, on the slope, or among brown trees,
Are grey and shrivelled. And the men who live here
Are small and withered, spider-like, with large eyes.

Bring water with you if you come to live here—
Cold tinkling cisterns, or else wells so deep
That one looks down to Ganges or Himalayas.
Yes, and bring mountains with you, white, moon-bearing,
Mountains of ice. You will have need of these
Profundities and peaks of wet and cold.

Bring also, in a cage of wire or osier,
Birds of a golden colour, who will sing
Of leaves that do not wither, watery fruits
That heavily hang on long melodious boughs
In the blue-silver forests of deep valleys.

I have now been here—how many years? Years unnumbered.
My hands grow clawlike. My eyes are large and starved.
I brought no bird with me, I have no cistern
Where I might find the moon, or river, or snow.
Some day, for lack of these, I'll spin a web
Between two dusty pine-tree tops, and hang there
Face downward, like a spider, blown as lightly
As ghost of leaf. Crows will caw about me.
Morning and evening I shall drink the dew.

Coleman Barks

A Section of the Oconee near Watkinsville

Before I get in,
the aluminum canoe floats flat on the shine
of water. Then I ruin its poise.
Middle of the first shoal though, I'm out,
stumbling through the ankle-breaking rocks.
Canoe free-floating downstream, without decision
or paddle. I lunge and bruise across the shallows
to get a forefinger in the rope eye on the stern.

June afternoon light. June afternoon water.

I know there's a life being led in lightness,
out of my reach and discipline.
I keep trying to climb in its words,
and so unbalance us both.
The teacher's example is everywhere open,
like a boat never tied up, no one in it,
that drifts day and night, metallic dragonfly
above the sunken log.

Hymenoptera

It's clinically wrong, but this begins with a drink,
alone, back from the Emergency Room, cortisone
in each hip, welts heating up in clusters
on right arm, chest, back, inside right thigh, left
shoulder, and between the eyelid and eyebrow,

twenty-one stings. I'm not sure
yellow jacket or hornet. Doctor says it doesn't matter,
both hymenoptera, *Little mean bastards,*
they go for the eyes.

A wonder of innocent membranous wings again
after six years, come to me not wandering, but in
my own remote meadow-yard, swingblading
what I take to be my duty of tall weeds. Now
days of itchy skinconsciousness, thankful
to be anywhere, burning to scratch blood. They smell me
with my venomous sensitivity, me especially.

I have heard what some objective someone said: *Coleman*
is riddled with fears. Well that may be,
and the problem then: to boil what mixture I have
into soup, a glad courage to be sipped as I walk
back without a shirt to retrieve the swingblade
where it fell, skin so awake to air
and any slight furry hair of bee that lights,
forerunner, pre-bee of swarm-to-come
that can't be fended off, the thought of which
mustn't. Last night this dream. A woman
lines up juice glasses, drinks for me, clear liquid.
In the bottom of each, under ice cubes, is a live,
moving-its-legs, bee. I'm expected to drink
the stingers down. I'm hesitating.

I didn't see what I hit in the grass that caused this.
Often it's clearer. I've known when I was swinging
into a hive-nest and gone on slow-motion
with a long swing. Make-happen and let-happen,
and other happens out of nowhere. I can't untangle
the green wire, but I know the feel of that sound
around my head. Swollen, blackening, and finally
patient, it gives me new eyes to see the lovely
obstructions, the bamboo scaffolding.

The air only seemed to be thickening into knots
that kill. I didn't foreknow these beestings.
I had the dream, but no clarity, the way now
I have angry bee-acid in me swelling
to circulate. Look at this line of drinks,
a future of juice glasses, each with a scarab
waking more and more in the melting
and the hesitation.

These are fearful gifts that I accept,
and cautiously hold to the light, and swallow,
biestings, the old word for the first milk,
which is clear, from the mother's breast.

Now you'll be crazy over bees, says Benjamin, Long Distance,
among my other fears of motorcycles, power tools, snakes
on low-hanging branches, and I summon them all
to let them hum around my head, one at a time.
I don't need another black hood of buzzing.
More than three, I hit the water quick,
and you can laugh if you want to.
I choose to watch my daylight panic as a rock does,
secretly covered-uncovered in the stream.

New Year's Day Nap

Fiesta Bowl on low.
My son lying here on the couch
on the "Dad" pillow he made for me
in the Seventh Grade. Now a sophomore
at Georgia Southern, driving back later today,
he sleeps with his white top hat over his face.
I'm a dancin' fool.

Twenty years ago, half the form
he sleeps within came out of nowhere
with a million micro-lemmings who all died but one
piercer of membrane, specially picked to start a brainmaking,
egg-drop soup, that stirred two sun and moon centers
for a new-painted sky in the tiniest
ballroom imaginable.

Now he's rousing, six feet long,
turning on his side. Now he's gone.

I sound low-key,
but this is the way I howl an old hymn
in the plaintive bass-drone,
a charm for accepting what happens,
and a stubborn question,

> *in the*
> *why   val-*
> *Say   ley*
> *of death   should weep*
> *Or   I*
> *lone   the   derness*
> *in   wil-*
> *rove?*

There's no one to worry about waking
with my singing. I have loved them,
those two boys, so well
that they've left.

We're after the fact now,
out in nowhere again.

We're I, and I am a line of music
wriggling along like water
waiting to be ocean.

               dars of Le-
        ce-   *ba-*   *bow*
The   *non*   *at*   *feet,*
                    with his
The   *is*   *fumed*
        air   per-
                              breath.

Singing and talking,
one vibrates with the other.
Vapor-mist-going-up-this-way,
cloud-come-back-around-down.

The old FaSoLa singers
would not commit to words,
until they ran through the notes,
in broken lines of rain.

The reverse of me rocking my babies
to all verses of Samanthra,
or *David's Lamentation,*
who now in a shower somewhere
murmur tunes they have no lyrics for.

La la   la
          sol   sol
     mi   mi   mi mi
            do

I never took them to church,
or told them stories about David,
or Samuel, or Jesus,
but they move like fish,
or tadpole-radios in the mud,
flat on their backs on a roof,
or breezing by.

Maybe any motion is holy music,
not only theirs.

Remember how it went,
then forget.

Sliding, forget more.
Sliding air in the throat, this song
it seems so soon to quit,
any shred of unfinished existence,

La la la
　　　　sol sol
　　　　　　　mi

that somehow
is unbelievably over.

The growing
　　　　　　of the
　　　　　　　　　corn

over and over.

Our watery bodies keep moving.

　　　　Hands give.

　　　　Eyes weep.

　　　　Feet walk,

　　　　Shoulders swim.

　　　　The throat sings.

　　　　The chest hopes.

The genitals wait.

And the thighs,

their small-stroke dancing work of balancing and lifting,
the thighs,
                    slow-move
a big riverlike forgiveness
we can jump in,
I and my strong boys, now men.

Some songs don't ever get completely sung.
They're sung by the blood,
inside creeks and rocks and air,
in some cellular Beulah land,
the harmonizing water sings them.

```
        do
     ti
fa          fa
      sol
            mi    mi                  mi
                re
                  do        do
                    ti  ti
              la          la          la
```

Roy Blount Jr.

Song to Okra

String beans are good, and ripe tomatoes,
And collard greens and sweet potatoes,
Sweet corn, field peas, and squash and beets—
But when a man rears back and *eats*
He wants okra.

Good old okra.

Oh wow okra, yessiree,
Okra is Okay with me.

Oh okra's favored far and wide,
Oh you can eat it boiled or fried,
Oh either slick or crisp inside,

Oh I once knew a man who died
Without okra.

Little pepper-sauce on it,
Oh! I wan' it:
Okra.

Old Homer Ogletree's so high
On okra he keeps lots laid by.
He keeps it in a safe he locks up.
He eats so much, can't keep his socks up.
(Which goes to show it's no misnomer

When people call him Okra Homer.)
Okra!

Oh you can make some gumbo wit' it,
But most of all I like to git it
All by itself in its own juice,
And lying there all nice and loose—
That's okra!

It may be poor for eating chips with,
It may be hard to come to grips with,
But okra's such a wholesome food
It straightens out your attitude.

"Mm!" is how discerning folk re-
Spond when they are served some okra.

Okra's green,
Goes down with ease.
Forget cuisine,
Say "Okra, please."

You can have strip pokra.
Give me a nice girl and a dish of okra.

Song to Grits

When my mind's unsettled,
When I don't feel spruce,
When my nerves get frazzled,
When my flesh gets loose—

What knits
Me back together's grits.

Grits with gravy,
Grits with cheese.
Grits with bacon,
Grits with peas.
Grits with a minimum
Of two over-medium eggs mixed in 'em: um!

Grits, grits, it's
Grits I sing—
Grits fits
In with anything.

Rich and poor, black and white,
Lutheran and Campbellite,
Southern Jews and Jesuits,
All acknowledge buttered grits.

Give me two hands, give me my wits,
Give me forty pounds of grits.

Grits at taps, grits at reveille.
I am into grits real heavily.

True grits,
More grits,
Fish, grits and collards.
Life is good where grits are swallered.

Grits
Sits
Right.

Song to Chitlins

Stop and think before belittlin'
That deeply visceral food, the chitlin.

Yes, it *is* a pork intestine.
Makes it specially interestin'.

You may find it infra dig,
But it worked wonders for the pig.

Adrienne Bond

Time Was, She Declares

—for Stephen W. Hawking

You may remember them too, the pictures
called TRANSPORTATION in those old geographies,
everything streamlined—car, truck, bus, plane,
train—hard-edged, in primary colors,
all moving off in different directions,
no one looking back or, missing someone,
suddenly starting to wave.
                                        She used
to read those books with great attention,
wondering *Wisconsin, Minnesota*—
the way a Jamaican might wonder *Miami*—
what it might be like in a place like that,
what she might have there.
                                        Summer days,
dazzled in the heat downtown, she'd lean
through the car window, watching
the trains roll, knowing
the bad thing about freight cars was,
as fast as she could read one, think
what it might be carrying,
carrying, it was gone, gone on.

II.
You've read about it, surely, the new
creation myth. She's heard (and entertains
the possibility it's true)
a point in time will come, taut

between bang and crunch, all silvery quiver
and in perfect tune, when reach
will momentarily equal grab,
and we will see the things we thought we'd lost
all pause, turn, and come avalanching
back—coins, lovers, kits and luggage,
teeth and keys and jobs,
umbrellas and the dead. She fears it,
freely admits that none of it
would match her memories: vignettes
fleshed out improbably, bold themes
disorienting back to random or routine, heavier
but of less import, and all those years
of storymaking gone for naught.

> *No,* she says.

III.
Think about this, she says. If we found out
that Elvis or, for that matter,
Jesus was expected to come through here,
say on a touring bike,
and somebody yelled,

> *There he goes,*

and we ran out and stood in the road
and watched those wheels grit up
the blacktop grade, spin down
between the peanuts and the corn,
roll past the knitting mill and on,
until far down the road we'd see
the shimmering pedals fall and rise,
move off along the ridgepole of the world
and out of sight—

> we'd put a good face
on it. We'd know how.

> She thinks
she'd probably check the mailbox then
as if that's what, for pity's sake,

we'd all gone out there for. We'd scatter,
each of us reading, with great attention,
anything that had our name on it,
anything at all.

Christmas Basket: 1943

"You need to come out home with me," grandmother said,
"to visit Mattie Wing." And so we went
rattling over the long plank bridges through the swamp,
where trees stood bare, out cold in tangles of wild grape,
and holly bristled in the wind.

"I always was her favorite," grandmother said.
"I should have done this months ago."

We drove so far in the country then,
bald wartime tires slick in the ruts,
I thought that we were lost. But there it was,
clapboards over logs, tin roof rust-splotched,
a dog trot boarded off to make a long dark hall,
and everything—pigs, chickens, turkeys—
running loose in the yard.

"She don't take nothing now but potlikker, sometimes
a little grits," the women whispered in the door.
And an old man in field clothes
got up out of his chair by the stove
and disappeared without a word
into the dim rooms at the back of the house.

We waited, not looking around. Hand
in hand, standing on ceremony,
we were smelling woodsmoke, fatback boiling.

Swaddled in quilts, a bundle of bones
like something an owl might drop, she sat
propped up in a highbacked wooden wheelchair,
distant as a star. "Old Girl," grandmother
wrung her hands, "I didn't mean for them
to get you out of bed."

We showed her the Johnson's oil, the bottle
of sweet wine, the corn meal, but her eyes were dull.
"This is Aurelia's child," grandmother told
the vacant face, "my namesake." Then,
turning to me, she asked, "Can you believe
the two of us climbed trees?" I shook my head.

Then the mouth pursed and slowly
a rusty voice commanded, "Tell her about
the time you thowed the hen in the well."
And grandmother cried out, "Oh,
I'll never live that down!"

And that was it. Afterwards, in the car,
I wondered, "Wasn't she glad we came?
She never even smiled." And grandmother said,
"Tell me one reason why she should,"
and hurled the old Ford down, down
between red clay banks, hands gripping the wheel,
eyes on the bad road home.

Burial

He set the pace, that relative
who needed neither map, nor path,
prospected down the fire ant infested
pipeline cut, across interminable rows

of pulpwood pines, wordless,
watching the ground for snakes;
and I, in sidewalk shoes but fixed
on finding my dead kin,
huffed to keep up.

Now you'll be interested
in this: we did find it
back in the paper company land
miles from anywhere, the pines
squared off outside the wrought iron fence
framing a small preserve
of wilderness, that green disorder
it was meant to hold at bay.
The gate, scrolled, rust-crusted,
opened into a fine old story,
all about lambs and angels, and
on the marble slabs, under the vines,
were legendary names.

My grandaddy said his mother
used to tell about the times
the dentist came and stayed a week
or more, grinding their teeth
with a foot-powered drill
and pounding gold in, flake by flake,
reciting famous speeches,
poetry or parts of plays. She said
they had to tie her brother to a chair.

I have imagined that boy,
red-faced with rage, and the
old dentist, foot pumping,
howling Hector round the walls
of Troy and Palinurus drowned
to kill the pain. Nothing

I ever really saw makes
such a hard-edged memory. I know
their nearest neighbors lived
in Buck Creek Swamp in something
like a pen; those people slept
on piles of straw and hunted
and ate clay. I do not know
my next door neighbor's name.

So there we were, my cousin
and I in the graveyard,
all that remained of what
was once the old home place.
I wish that I could say
their shades came crowding up
wailing, indistinguishable now
from those pot-hunters and
their slattern wives memorialized
for a while by piled dirt,
a broken dish. But under that oak
were only earth and rock and root;
no gold gleamed in its old limbs.

Here Martha Lockhart and John Murray
Green lie boxed up still, boxed
in, stiff in their city clothes.
They do not see humor in it,
nor do I. There is a faint
but unmistakable whiff in the wind,
the sulphur breath of that necessity
which owns them now, which,
by agreement, had to leave
a clearing here, but not a road.

On the Fall Line

> What did you go out
> to the wilderness to see?
> A reed shaken by the wind?
> —Matthew 11:7

God knows it's reasonable
to love a life
that's shaped to our desire, need,
whatever, but we don't.

Like at the new mall
where fall comes in by truck,
cool air, piped music,
harvest home and all;
and never mind outside
a sun like hellfire
softens the asphalt.

So now and then,
going home, we ease
out of line, stop
at a country store
for beer and take
the old road to the river.

And we leave our shoes
on the floorboard, walk
through mud and weeds down
to the bank, slap gnats
and watch what's out there.

And the beer cans bump down
one by one
past shoals and strainers,
down to the drop-off

where the world's old bones
show through,
and the river seems to wash
the tics and twitches
of our lives away,
and we tell ourselves
that we'll come back here
Sunday, bring the dog
or some of the children,
but we won't.

　　　　　We know
that after a while this place
gets on our nerves as bad
as any other place; that
the sounds of the water
become as tiresome,
finally, as the sounds
of our own voices,
as mindless
as the music at the mall.

David Bottoms

Free Grace at Rose Hill

My uncle found it in a crater on Bloody Ridge
and stepped off a troop ship into Riverdale Baptist.
I heard it off his tongue
crackling like an open fire,
Love is fire. And once in remote mountains
at the church of a cousin, I heard
that sizzle in a wooden box a man had thrust his hand into.
What came up writhing in his fist
coiled above him like a sequined halo.

This was all argument, proof. I listened
my whole boyhood
and my listening couldn't save me.

But maybe you've walked on a Sunday in your favorite woods
and heard through the shuffling of leaves
the distant rustle of tongues, the handclapping,
the stirring of feet,
or the single inspired voice singing over a thunder of fans,

and maybe, like me, you paused once in the dogwoods
at the edge of that churchyard
to hear the many tongues rendering into one
the promise of an old hymn
and felt yourself listening suddenly
with your heart.

No, that wasn't grace either,
though grace had been there—
Isn't it like this cemetery where the roses

quaking in their terraces are not the wind?
It swirls where it wants to swirl.
If it touches us,
it touches us.

Snake on the Etowah

Kicking through woods and fields, I'd spooked several
and once stepped on a coachwhip among gravestones,
at least one garter curled like a bow
under ivy in my yard.
Once I even woke on the hazy bank of a lake,
wiped dew from my eyes and found
on my ankle
a cottonmouth draped like a bootlace.

I thought I knew how beauty could poison
a moment with fear,
but wading that low river, feet wide on rocks—
my rod hung on the backswing, my jitterbug
snagged on the sun—
I felt something brush my thigh.
The bronze spoon of a copperhead drifted
between my legs.

Out came the little tongue reaching
in two directions,
the head following upriver,
following down, then a wide undulation of tail,
a buff and copper swish. The river eased
around it in a quivering V,
while inside my shudder
it slipped out—
spiny, cool, just below
the surface, sidling against the current.

Shooting Rats at the Bibb County Dump

Loaded on beer and whiskey, we ride
to the dump in carloads
to turn our headlights across the wasted field,
freeze the startled eyes of rats against mounds of rubbish.

Shot in the head, they jump only once, lie still
like dead beer cans.
Shot in the gut or rump, they writhe and try to burrow
into garbage, hide in old truck tires,
rusty oil drums, cardboard boxes scattered across the mounds,
or else drag themselves on forelegs across our beams of light
toward the darkness at the edge of the dump.

It's the light they believe kills.
We drink and load again, let them crawl
for all they're worth into the darkness we're headed for.

Coasting toward Midnight at the Southeastern Fair

Stomach in my throat
I dive on rails and rise like an astronaut,
orbit this track like mercury sliding
around a crystal ball.
Below me a galaxy of green and blue neon
explodes from the midway to Industrial Boulevard,
and red taillights comet one after another
down the interstate toward Atlanta.

In the hot dog booth the Lions are sick of cotton candy.
Along the midway Hercules feels the weight of his profession,
Mother Dora sees no future
in her business,

the tattooed lady questions the reason
behind each symbol drawn indelibly beneath her flesh.

We all want to break our orbits,
float like a satellite gone wild in space,
run the risk of disintegration.
We all want to take our lives in our own hands
and hurl them out among the stars.

Recording the Spirit Voices

In the hollow below the hill vaults
I have placed a recorder
on the grave of a young woman killed in a fire
and have crouched under the arm of this angel
to wait for voices,
tree frogs whirring through the blue pines,
the Ocmulgee lapping the bank at the foot of Rose Hill.

A gray moon over the Confederate graves
gleams on the water,
the white gallon jugs floating some man's trotline.
Like me, he's trying to bring things to the surface
where they don't belong.

And across the river
blue needles rasp like the voices
I heard on television,
the documented whisper of spirits, *I'm afraid here, I'm afraid.*
So am I now
as leaves in the hollow rustle their dry tongues:
afraid to hear a woman scream from a burning house,
to record some evidence her tombstone lied,
bury the truth these angels stand on: *born* and *died.*

In a U-Haul North of Damascus

1:
Lord, what are the sins
I have tried to leave behind me? The bad checks,
the workless days, the Scotch bottles thrown across the fence
and into the woods, the cruelty of silence,
the cruelty of lies, the jealousy,
the indifference?

What are these on the scale of sin
or failure
that they should follow me through the streets of Columbus,
the moon-streaked fields between Benevolence
and Cuthbert where dwarfed cotton sparkles like pearls
on the shoulders of the road? What are these
that they should find me half-lost,
sick and sleepless
behind the wheel of this U-Haul truck parked in a field on Georgia 45
a few miles north of Damascus,
some makeshift rest stop for eighteen wheelers
where the long white arms of oaks slap across trailers
and headlights glare all night through a wall of pines?

2:
What was I thinking, Lord?
That for once I'd be in the driver's seat, a firm grip
on direction?

So the jon boat muscled up the ramp,
the Johnson outboard, the bent frame of the wrecked Harley
chained for so long to the back fence,
the scarred desk, the bookcases and books,
the mattress and box springs,
a broken turntable, a Pioneer amp, a pair
of three-way speakers, everything mine
I intended to keep. Everything else abandon.

But on the road from one state
to another, what is left behind nags back through the distance,
a last word rising to a scream, a salad bowl
shattering against a kitchen cabinet, china barbs
spiking my heel, blood trailed across the cream linoleum
like the bedsheet that morning long ago
just before I watched the future miscarried.

Jesus, could the irony be
that suffering forms a stronger bond than love?

3:
Now the sun
streaks the windshield with yellow and orange, heavy beads
of light drawing highways in the dew-cover.
I roll down the window and breathe the pine-air,
the after-scent of rain, and the far-off smell
of asphalt and diesel fumes.

But mostly pine and rain
as though the world really could be clean again.

Somewhere behind me,
miles behind me on a two-lane that streaks across
west Georgia, light is falling
through the windows of my half-empty house.
Lord, why am I thinking about this? And why should I care
so long after everything has fallen
to pain that the woman sleeping there should be sleeping alone?
Could I be just another sinner who needs to be blinded
before he can see? Lord, is it possible to fall
toward grace? Could I be moved
to believe in new beginnings? Could I be moved?

Edgar Bowers

Spaces

Of spaces there are many, outer, inner
Positives in the void, like destinies
Mysterious and absolute, where quarks
And relatives of quarks play host to shape.
And though there is a chip set in the brain
Mathematical and kin to them, there are
Other evaluations as a truth,
Joy honoring right sacrifices, grief
Certain to come whenever we will call,
And peace, that is a Parthenon of shapes.
Suppose we take a *Voyager* to Neptune,
Another hazard in uncertainty,
The discipline of wonder, and we see
Volcanoes breathing glaciers, rainless clouds
Shadowing other clouds, and Triton again
Offshore in blue and silver tides, there, too,
The lover that is in us will exclaim,
Both cameraman and painter, "It is good!"
For though the art of love repeats the same
Final epistemologies, we know
The time that we must travel brings us back
Inescapably to where there is no space,
Perspective keener for the vanishing.
"The wheel has come full circle," Edmund sighs,
"And I am here at last, eternally,"
Who would have been a lover, had he known.

Numbers

"Odd, divine and mysterious numbers"—Rabelais

Though the order of real numbers seem enough
For astronauts, as it seemed once for him
Who, from an apple's sudden fall, inferred
A universe at poise; though business men,
Through all the sums from nine to zero, add
And multiply their hopes and fears; and though
Musicians, when they play duets and trios,
Be satisfied with their Pythagoras,
Each of them, should he contemplate desire,
Its spins and its velocities, its racy
Particles and unlinear lines, will need
Imaginary numbers. Often I
Rely on fortune for a metaphor
Like that of our first meeting, you a presence
Mysterious as the first bright precedent
And I three old dimensions to a point—
That primitive geometry! But only
Minuses to extraordinary powers
Approach, of our invisibilities,
The altered ways of seeming and unforeseen
Disequilibriums caused by time and chance,
The comedy renewed like outer space,
Black holes, new suns, replenished galaxies—
The state of less than zero that is love;
Though where we once have been and where we go
Be like another voyage to the moon
Or Phaëton's ashes scattered on the dark,
Dissonances that have no resolution
Or nature's ripeness scented by its bruises.

Van K. Brock

Novas

Who called flowers "mouths"?—these painted lips
of mimes frozen in imperceptible motion. Azaleas
hold the pose for days, weeks in temperate weather—
such reds, whites and purples, I lose my thread—
whispering essences, mouths that mock speech
with stillness, composing fuchsia symphonies
with fragrances so thin one is only an eighth note,
but here are the banks and reeds of Arcadia.

They surround me: I am theirs: wifewarp, childwoof,
birdflower, cloudtree. The porches of the poor
are propped up by azaleas. I am wrapped in woods.
The mouths say, *I am hungry.* They say, *Hum a thin song.*
In my yard, under a bush, the anthill streams red
stingers in and out. A city of law and industry.
All day and night their armies march to and from
their catacombs. I think they never sleep.

At night, when I fly into Los Angeles, spread
like a cancer of wisteria on the crumbling edge
of the continent, even its slums seem luminous.
Mouths! Mouths! What are they saying? The ripened
slums say, *Police are a state of mind, and we are
their colonies.* Just before dawn, after the rain
has washed the air, a pimp—raped, beaten, and OD'd—
comes to and sees his whore beside him, her throat cut,

the sky afloat with brilliant bones. Words of ash
and fire: star orchids and those black stellar flowers
forever collapsing inward and exploding outward in
rhythms that rock firmly in the center of yourself:
listen! They begin and end the long curve of eternity.
I am knocking on a wooden table in a dark seance.
Viewed from the moon, looking back, Earth's blue
anthill throbbing like an orchid in a vast austerity

of fireants that have vaulted the woods of imagining:
here all worlds that ever existed still exist in an eye
for which time is merely the spatial lines of perspective,
and Plato, Dante, Einstein are silent red songs on a bush,
interlocking cones of perception, sequential, burning
together, telling what the stars say, what azaleas mime,
while I am trying to hear the song enabling the ant
with its load of contraband pollen to lift thrice its weight.

Kathryn Stripling Byer

All Hallows Eve

I go by taper of cornstalk,
the last light of fields wreathed in woodsmoke,
to count the hens left in the chickenhouse
raided by wild dogs and foxes.
Our rooster crows far up the hillside
where three piles of rocks mark the graves
of nobody I ever knew.
Let their ghosts eat him!
Each year they grow hungrier,
wanting the squash run to seed in our garden,
the tough spikes of okra. Tonight while the moon
lays her face on the river and begs
for a love song, they'll come down the mountain
to steal the last apples I've gathered.

They'll stand at the window and ask us
for whom is that buttermilk set on the table?
That platter of cold beans?
They know we will pay them no heed.
It's the wind, we will say,
watching smoke sidle out of the fireplace,
or hearing the cellar door rattle.

No wonder they go away
always complaining how little the living
have learned, on our knees
every night asking God for a clean heart,
a pure spirit. Spirit? They kick
up the leaves round the silent house.

What good is spirit without hands for walnut
to stain, without ears for the river
to fill up with promises? What good,
they whisper, returning to nothing, what good
without tongue to cry out to the moon,
"Thou hast ravished my heart, O my sister!"

Hawk

Up here I am safe.
There's no need they should come.
Let them sweat at their stoves,
stirring mayhaws until the juice spins
a red thread. Let them cherish the jars
on their shelves. I was never their fool.
Rainbows end in the mud where
I come from. No wind, and the clouds
stay so long they grow yellow
as old satin curtains nobody can open
or wants to, for nothing is out there
but windmills that won't move
or corn that won't grow. It's no good
for a woman. That stillness.
How long have I been gone? A hundred
years? Grandmother prayed I'd come
home and my mother said I'd live
to curse my contrariness. Ha,
I curse women who won't live
to hear the wind blow all night long
as it does over Cherokee Gap. I will
never go back. Can't they understand that?
I do not want their peach wine,
their jelly too thick to be spooned.
God forbid I should ever eat fruitcake again!
Here they come up that road like a caravan

out of the flatlands, with tears
in their eyes and their lips puckered
round their sweet words. But I swear
by that hawk I see biding its time
over Warwoman Ridge I will not iron
my black dress and wear my hair tight
in a bun. I will not throw the first clod
of dirt in the hole. Lock the door,
girl, and tell them there's nobody home.

The Backwoods

Great-grandmother carried the cadence of Genesis.
Girl cousins up late at family reunions,
we made her an Indian, although her forebears
were Irish. Before her lay darkness, the empty fields
barren as desert until she came forward,
the sweat on her high cheekbones gleaming like eyes
we imagined surrounding her, bob-cat and red fox,
the last of the sleek, singing wolves. Every evening
she shouldered her hoe and walked home
through the tasselling corn. The Good Lord only knows
what bare feet stalked the backwoods in those days,
what waited behind every woodpile! She brought forth
a daughter with black hair that never curled.
Shy as a fieldmouse, that girl fell in love
with a man scything hay in the twilight. They kissed
twice. A moment she stood in her white dress
and smiled back at us, then she grew fat and sighed
in the kitchen. Four daughters she bore,
and the three who survived scarlet fever
wove grass in their brown hair and danced every night
with the fireflies. They galloped on wild horses
bareback until they got married and gave birth

to us, Southern Belles who could sit in a parlor
all evening and never complain. We could faint
in a handsome man's arms. We could charm
a stone wall. But we never forgot the back door,
how to disappear into the darkness, our crinolines rustling
like cornstalks between our legs. We told
this story so well, we inherit its black earth
where women hoe all night, inscrutable as Indians.

For Jim on Siler's Bald

Dizzy with you on the edge,
after what seemed like hours of climbing
toward sunlight, I stepped
back and studied a hawk floating
over the valley like a kite

somebody let go of. Why speak
of life changing its seasons
again? How the hardwoods
bore leaves into view or
the bears brushed off sleep
like a cobweb to follow the light
growing long on the leafmold
where earthworms fished,
busy as fingers? That happened

as always. But wind?
I remember the hawk riding
on it to nowhere I knew
when we lay down in thin air
to sleep with the rest of the creatures
the earth was about to awaken.

Thieves

Take all you want,
she'd say, slicing the biggest cabbage
or filling a sack with too many tomatoes.
Her husband was taken away on a stretcher
that creaked, dressed in new silk pajamas
and sealed in a coffin. The next day she moved
to town, jungle of ferns and her four-poster bed
in the back of a pick-up truck. Thieves came
to loot the abandoned house, little
by little took all her old clothes, even took
her pressed rose petals crumbling in cheap Zane Grey novels.
They left many cigarette butts to burn holes

in her carpet and frighten us when we came back
every month to the homeplace. Were they in her bedroom
that night the hail pounded her tin roof
and shattered her window panes? Any thief
rifling her coat pockets should have gone down on his knees
as if he'd heard the sky of the last judgment falling,

what she herself must have believed
when lightning awakened her, slumped
in her armchair, the TV still going.
The picture was ripping apart with each blast.
(I remember the rending of sheets every April,
her bed full of rags, and how she caressed dull wood
for days until she made it kindle with light

through her brocaded windows.) Next morning
we drove her out to the rubble that still smoked.
She walked to the edge of it,
stirring the ruins with her walking stick,
looking for something.
Nobody knew what.

"Nothing there," she said,
prodding the broken glass,
blackened stone under her feet.
"They took it all," she explained
to us, nodding her head
like a child. "I knew they would."

Turner Cassity

The New Dolores Leather Bar

> I adjure thee, respond from thine altars,
> Our Lady of Pain.
> —A.C. Swinburne

Not quite alone from night to night you'll find them.
Who need so many shackles to remind them
Must doubt that they are prisoners of love.

The leather creaks; studs shine; the chain mail jingles.
Shoulders act as other forms of bangles
In a taste where push has come to shove.

So far from hardhats and so near to Ziegfeld,
They, their costume, fail. Trees felled, each twig felled,
One sees the forest: Redneck Riding Hood's.

Does better-dear-to-eat-you drag, with basket,
Make the question moot? Go on and ask it.
Red, do you deliver, warm, the goods?

Or is the axle-grease, so butch an aura,
Underneath your nails in fact mascara?
Caution, lest you lie, your skin unscarred,

Profane these clanking precincts of the pain queen.
Numb with youth, an amateur procaine queen,
In the rite you lose the passage. Hard,

To know the hurt the knowledge. Command is late now,
Any offer master of your fate now.
You can, though won't, escape. Tarnishing whore,

So cheap your metal and so thin your armor,
Fifteen years will have you once more farmer.
Mammon values; earth and pain ignore.
Name your price and serve him well before.

The Chinaberry Tree

Its shape uncertain in the bloom that scrims it,
Purple, and itself a haze of gnats,
The tree that will be knowledge, or what seems it,
Beckons in the rising heat and waits.

Its shade will feather, and be serpent; there,
Instinct to take the field and meet the beast,
Are bound, already bargainers, a pair
On whom the subtleties will all be lost.

The altered apple, as if randomly,
Exerts its blunt appeal, and though who fall
Acquire a taste, it is not learning. Try,
Avenger, angel posted, as you will.

The sword that flames exile shows up to be
Dessert stuck on a skewer, and the taint
Of Adam, late and early, gluttony.
How tartly, as the sandflies learn, the faint,

Soft blossoms harden in their unmeant Eden
Toward the green, emetic berry: scent
Nil, outline clear—late come-on for a want
Too uninformative to seem forbidden.

Other Directed

Two roads diverge, each in a yellow smog.
It is the Freeway. I? I take the one
Most traveled by. It makes no difference,
Nor should it. Eight wide lanes and well-marked turns
Will get you there, without the waste and mud,
Ornate delays of detours. If you know—
Mind, really know—so late itinerant,
Where you are going, is there, now and then,
Some reason not to take the easy way?

In the land of great aunts

I
Making Blackberry Jelly
In gallon cans, the berries fill the kitchen:
One of red to eight of ripe. Escutcheon,

Challenge of the wholly confident,
Her labels—dated, as if vintage meant—

Already mark the glasses. Never once
The aid of Sure-Jell, 'never once one ounce

To turn to sugar.' White, the cotton sacks
Await that purple they will strain. Attacks

(Appendicitis) come from eating seeds,
And jam does not quite suit the artist's needs:

The primal urge to seal in paraffin
Some essence wholly clarified. Thick, thin,

Remain the juices all which they have been.
The loose white blossom on the pale green vine;

These tiny chandeliers as dark as wine.
Clustering seed-pearls turned to red, the time

Of ripeness, and the other time of dread—
The liquid flood of birth; its jelling dead.

Pour out the total, for the rest is chance;
Pectin will shape now, or ferment advance.

Seal! Tyrian purple is from cotton wrung;
The whole of sense is gathered on the tongue.

II
Costuming the Pageant
The neat fire falters in the polished grate;
The treadle, oiled and mute, fails at such rate

As daylight and the ankle fail. Stout seamstress,
Is the robe you sew your one remonstrance—

Satin, tinsel—for this winter room
And year round solitude? Or in that tome

(The Doré Bible) open on your Singer
Is the pattern all: a wire coat-hanger

Bent for halo, cheesecloth cut for wings.
And if each host that with the angel sings

May also be, aloft in close formation,
Lucifer and cohorts, age and gumption

Are the lance to keep him still at bay.
Now, on her fingers—late—community

Has marked its own. Tenacious brass, the tinsel
Stains. Out of season, not the cup and chancel,

Yet communion all the same. She takes,
Receiver, giver of the gift she makes:

A gold, a frankincense of usefulness,
And myrrh of old achievement, strong to bless.

The practiced poker will command the embers;
Out of the treadle will the angel come.

III
Visiting the Cemetery
Who of these ordered dead, the named and grouped,
Has lost particularity? Descript,

If curtly, dated by the mason's art,
They form a whole of which she knows each part:

A branching genealogy in stone.
The stone tree flowers; the lineal, made one

In floral line with the collateral,
Have each the bloom her yard-man puts on all—

The eighteen small glass jars, as many flowers.
Upright, the yard-man stoops. His mistress towers.

Afternoon is quiet, and is not;
As if the dead were so much unforgot

They had a far, familiar pulse. Again,
Again, the sawmill sounds and is the kin.

If, when Negro tends her grave as well
(It being somehow tacit that he will);

If her stone means to no one, least to him,
Well-being and warm continuum,

Do these consanguine join the non-descript?
The lumber says deny, the shade accept.

Between, the dead are what they were. For what they are,
The early jonquil glistens in the mason jar.

Pearl Cleage

Can You See Them?

I been ridin through America
like an orphan child
with no momma's lap
no Christmas tree,
no daddy's arms
to hide in, glide in, slide in
and wait out the storm.

I been ridin through America
stomach full of rum-spiked coffee
and ice cold beer. Stomach full
of Eggs McMuffin and Quarter Pounders
with cheese.

I been ridin through America,
lookin at Tennessee,
listenin to Kentucky,
crossin the Ohio River on the run,
even though I don't have to anymore,
no matter what they say,
or how loud they say it.

I been ridin through America,
ears on fire like nobody's child,
and everybody's b/a/b/y,
singin that country song
where the woman says:
Cuz I still love you,
or at least I think I do.

And we laugh at how free we feel,
out together, ridin through America,
and then we round the curve
of that mountain road
and we gasp and holler
at the beauty of the land,
and it makes us love each other more.
It makes us love our children
and our mothers and our fathers,
and our grandmothers,
and our grandfathers,
more and more and more and more . . .

Sometimes we think we see our ancestors
walking up these rivers
in the mist. Sometimes we try
not to talk about it.
But then he will say:
Can you see them?
Dropping his voice like spirits
can't hear all the way down
into your very soul
even if you whisper.

Can you see them?

And I want to tell him:
No, I don't see anything.
Can't you see I'm busy
ridin through America?
But: Yes, I say. Oh, yes,
I see them. I always see them.

Sometimes their presence makes us
want to pledge something.
We want to promise to always
do thus and so, forever and forever,

to the absolute grave and beyond
where there is only energy and light
and wind and then the stillness.

Sometimes their presence makes us
weep and cuss and wonder
how and when and where and why
they died here. And how come
when they told Beulah Mae Donald
that the Klan had lynched her son
in downtown Mobile, Alabama on March 21, 1981,
she closed her eyes and thanked her god

because at least they hadn't thrown
his mutilated body into the river.
And what kind of something is that
to be thankful for?

Nobody wants to think about race
all the damn time.
Even me. Especially me.
I'd rather think about love,
and how to get hold of that picture
my sister has of my mother,
looking like a bohemian intellectual,
glasses perched on the bridge of her nose,
cigarette dangling from her longer-
than-I-remember-them fingers.
I'd rather think about my fat little nephew
blinking up into his first snow,
and my Uncle Louis' poem
about the high bouncing lover
in the bright gold hat.

I said nobody wants to think about race
all the damn time.

I hadn't seen that face for a week,
but I recognized it instantly.
The way his skin stretches over the bones

like it's about to tear. The eyes.
We've only been back in the city one day
and he is already pacing.

No, I say, teasing, trying
to make him smile, hugging him tighter than I meant to:
You can't go and you can't move.
That's what they all say, he says,
and moves my arms from around his neck
and moves my arms from around his neck.
Openness to me is openness to them,
and we all know the penalty for that.

Better to close the house, pack a bag,
check the tires and hit the road.
It's harder to hit a moving target anyway,
which is why I been ridin through America,
runnin through America,
tryin to pretend it's Christmas,
and hopin this time
the river won't be so cold
and we can make it all the way to Canada.

Mixed Drink

(for Kalia)

Her father used to park her
around the corner from the liquor store
so she wouldn't see him going in
and have to lie to her grandmother.

Her mother taught her
how to make Manhattans
and died at home in bed
with a boyfriend who had
no experience in such matters
and greeted the fact of it
by screaming naked in the street
until the police came
and took charge of things.

Now she wants to tell her stories.
She dips her pen
in memories and vermouth
and mixes them well.

At the Warwick Hotel

At the Warwick Hotel,
the desk clerk drinks,
the waitresses play the numbers
and they lock the door at midnight.
Late arrivals are greeted
with minor curiosity
and a blast of gin.

Judith Ortiz Cofer

Before the Storm

(Hurricane Luis, Puerto Rico, 1995)

We are talking in whispers
about what is worth saving. A box of photographs
is pushed under the bed, and the rendering
of Jesus knocking at somebody's door, a hesitant young man,
that arrived with us in each new house, and another
of his dear mother holding his poor broken body
not many years later, are taken down
from their precarious places on the walls.
We surprise each other with our choices.

She fills boxes
while I watch the sky for signs, though I feel,
rather than see, nature is readying
for the scourge. Falling silent, the birds seek safety
in numbers, and the vagabond dogs cease their begging
for scraps. The avocados are dropping
from the laden trees in her backyard
as if by choice. Bad weather always brings in a good crop
of the water-fruit, she tells me; it is the land
offering us a last meal.

On the outer islands, the fragile homes of the poor
are already in its jaws, the shelters we see on film,
all those bodies huddled in the unnatural dark, the wind howling
like a hungry dog in the background, make us stand solemn.
In the mainland my family and friends will watch
the satellite pictures of this storm with trepidation
as it unravels over the Caribbean. But I am already too close
to see the whole picture. Here, there is

a saturated mantle descending,
a liquid fullness in the air, like a woman feels
before the onset of labor. Finally,
the growing urgency of the sky, and I am strangely excited,
knowing that I am as ready as I will ever be,
should I have another fifty years to go,
to go with my mother
towards higher ground. And when we come home, if
we come home, if there's a home where we believe
we left one, it will all be different.

Notes for My Daughter Studying Math on the Morning of a New Year

Mira, mira, our Spanish speaking kin
are always saying. Look and look again. It amuses us,
this insistence on seeing, even when they mean listen.
Could it be that they keep the world less at bay
than we their exiled children? That they can see
emotions in color? Anger is the scarlet
hibiscus; joy the blue of the Puerto Rican sky
after a July rainstorm, and grief,
a black mantilla on the head of the woman
sitting alone in the last pew of an empty church.
Mira, hija, I say to you in my mother's voice,
when I mean listen, and you may turn your eyes
in the direction of some unexpected bit of wonder:
the dull gray city pigeon is iridescent
in a certain slant of light, and she perches
at *your* window. If this is not enough, pues, mira,
the sun shines indiscriminately over everything. Mira.
Even the shadows make interesting designs on the concrete.

Listen: whatever the weather, when you step outside
and breathe deeply, you inhale the history
of our race in each molecule: Eve's desire,
Cleopatra's ambition, Magdalene's guilt,
the New World of Isabel of Castile,
the fierce conquests of Elizabeth, and the genius
of Sor Juana and Virginia Woolf; here too remains,
the labored breath of an old woman
fishing a day's meal at the dumpster,
and the fears of the fourteen year old run-away
who will soon run out of breath; my own relief
as the nurse settled you in my arms
on the day you arrived
into the breathless world.

Try to speak
in Spanish in your dreams. Say sol,
día, sueños, as you fall asleep. See
if you can believe that tomorrow
may be the day you have been designing in the dark,
an algebra from particles of light
swirling behind your eyelids—
your own private theory of relativity.

First Job: The Southern Sweets Sandwich Shop and Bakery

Lillie Mae glows, she hates the word *sweat,*
as she balances a platter of baked sweets over her head,
showing me how to walk with grace
even under the weight of minimum wage
and a mountain of cookies,
turnovers, and tarts which she blames
for her "voluptuous" figure. She calls me
"shuggah," and is teaching me the job.

We are both employed by Mr. Raymond, who keeps her
in a little house outside of town.

I'm fifteen, living my first year
in the strange country called Georgia.
Lillie Mae hired me for my long black hair
she couldn't wait to braid, and for my gift
of tongues, which she witnessed as I turned
my mother's desire for a sugar bubble
she called a *merengue* into something nearly equal
behind the glass wall.

"Shuggah," she will on occasion call me
out front, "talk foreign for my friend."
And I will say whatever comes into my head,
"You're a pig, Mr. Jones, I see your hand
under the table stroking her thigh." If they're impressed
with my verbal prowess, may I suggest something tasty
from our menu; if they presume I'm Pocahontas
at the palace, there only to amuse their royal selves,
I tell them, smiling sweetly, to try the *mierda*
which is especially good that day. Soon I can make
anything sound appetizing in Spanish.

Lillie Mae carries her silver-plated tray
to Mr. Raymond for inspection, looking seductive
as a plump Salome in her fitted white nylon uniform.
He is a rotund King Herod asking for the divinity
though he knows it's on its way. She sorts her delicacies,
pointing out the sugar-coated wedding cookies with the tips
of her pink glue-on nails she's so proud of.
"Because, Shuggah, a woman's hands should always
be soft and beautiful, never mind you scrubbed, waxed,
pushed, pulled, and carried all blessed day.
That's what a man expects."

I watch them as they talk shop and lock eyes,
but can't quite imagine the carnivale of their couplings.
Instead I see them licking their chops over strudel,
consuming passion while ensconced in her edible house
with peppermint stick columns and gingerbread walls.

In the kitchen of the Southern Sweets the black cook,
Margaret, worships at the altar of her Zenith radio. Hank Aaron
is working his way to heaven. She is bone-sticking thin,
despises sweets, loves only her man Hank, Otis Redding,
and a smoke. She winks at me when he connects,
dares to ignore Mr. Raymond when Aaron is up. Mysteriously
the boss-man understands the priority of home-runs,
and the sacrilege of speaking ordinary words like my
"triple decker club on a bun with fries" frozen at tongue-tip
when Margaret holds up one bony finger at us, demanding
a little respect for the man at the plate.

That windowless kitchen, with its soul-melting
hot floors and greasy walls had to disappear for her,
like a magician's trick at the sweet snap of the ball and bat
that sent her into orbit, her eyes rolling back in ecstasy,
mouth circling the O in wonder as if she had seen the glory.

At closing, Lillie Mae fluffs her boot-black curls,
heads home to entertain her sugar-daddy or to be alone,
glue-on new nails, pin-curl her hair and practice walking
gracefully under heavy trays.

I have home-work to do, words to add to my arsenal
of sweet-sounding missiles for mañana.

My father waits for me in his old brown Galaxy.
He's wary of these slow-talking tall Southerners, another race
he must avoid or face; tired of navigating his life,
which is a highway crowded with strangers sealed in their vehicles, and

badly marked with signs that he will never fully understand.
I offer him a day-old doughnut, but no, at least from me
he doesn't have to accept second-best anything.

we drive by the back lot where Margaret stands
puffing small perfect clouds, her eyes fixed to a piece of sky
between the twin smoke-stacks of Continental Can, and beyond
what I can see from where I am. Still tracking Aaron's message
hovering above us all in the air-waves?
Her lips move and I can read the drawled-out, "shee-it"
followed by that characteristic shake of her head
that meant, Girl, in this old world,
some things are still possible.

Where You Need to Go

A visit home to Puerto Rico, 1994

My life began here in this pueblo
now straining against its boundaries
and still confused about its identity:
Spanish village or tourist rest-stop,
with its centuries-old church
where pilgrims on their knees beg
a dark madonna for a miracle,
then go to lunch at Burger King.

Here is the place
where I first wailed for life
in a pre-language understood by all
in the woman-house where I was born,
where absent men in military uniform
paraded on walls alongside calendars
and crosses; and telegrams were delivered
by frightened adolescent boys

who believed all coded words from Korea
were about death. But sometimes
they were just a "Bueno, Mujer,"
to the women who carried on
their blood duties on the home-front.

I know this place,
although I've been away most of my life.
I've never really recovered
from my plunge, that balmy February day,
into the unsteady hands
of the nearly blind midwife,
as she mumbled prayers in Latin
to the Holy Mother, who had Herself
been spared the anguish
this old woman witnessed all those years;
to the aroma of herbal teas
brewed for power in *la lucha,* and the haunting
of the strangely manic music
that accompanies both beginnings
and endings here. I absorbed it all
through my pores. It remains
with me still, as a vague urge
to reconnect.

Today, opening my eyes again
in my mother's house,
I know I will experience certain things
that come to me in dreams, and déjà vu,
and memory: the timeless tolling of bells,
because time must be marked for mortal days
in seconds and in measured intervals,
to remind them as they drink their morning *café*
that they will die; the rustling of palm fronds
against venetian blinds, kitchen sounds
from my childhood; and muffled words

I cannot quite decipher, spoken in a language
I now have to translate, like signs
in a foreign airport you recognize
as universal symbols, and soon
their true meaning will come to you. It must.
For this is the place where you decide
where you need to go.

The Dream of Birth

Her voice as familiar as my own,
scrapes the ocean floor,
coming through ragged with static during the call
from Puerto Rico. She is staying at her sister's house
until she finds a new place for herself—has called
to say she is moving again and to share the horror
prompting her flight.

On the first night of deep sleep in the old house
she had rented back on native soil—a place
she would decorate with our past, where
yellowed photographs of a young man in khaki
army issue (the way she chooses to remember her husband)
and my brother and me as sepia-toned babies in their chipped frames,
a place where she could finally begin to collect
her memories like jars of preserves on a shelf—
there, she had lain down to rest on her poster bed centered
in a high-ceilinged room, exhausted from the labor
of her passage, and dreamed
she had given birth to one of us again. She felt the weight
of a moist, wriggling mass on her chest, the greedy mouth
seeking a milk-heavy breast, then suddenly—real pain—

piercing as a newborn infant's cry—yanking her
out of her dream. In the dark she felt the awful heft
of the thing stirring over her. Flipping on the light

she saw, to her horror, a bat clinging to her gown,
its hallucinated eyes staring up from the shroud of black wings,
hanging on, hanging on, with perfect little fingers,
                                            as she,
wild with fear and revulsion, struggled free of her clothes,
throwing the bundle hard against the wall. By daylight
she had returned to find the rust-colored stain streaked
on the white plaster, and the thing still fluttering
in the belly of the dress. She had dug a tiny grave
with her gardening spade on the spot
where she would have planted roses.

Stephen Corey

Attacking the Pietà

> On May 21, 1972, Michelangelo's Vatican *Pietà* was
> assaulted by Lazlo Toth, 33, a Hungarian-born
> Australian geologist who scaled a marble balustrade
> in St. Peter's Basilica and lashed out with a hammer,
> crying "I am Jesus Christ!"

1. Michelangelo Begins
His first blow to the block shows nothing
yet still is a start toward shape—
thought to thing, edge to curve,
world from the hard, blank earth.
The one piece of his life
on which he will carve his name.
Spurred by his fear of the graven image,
of the easy ways the righteous go astray
when thought and act diverge,
he guides the perfect slab into perfection.

2. New York World's Fair, 1964
When I was sixteen, I gave in
to my parents' hands steering my shoulders
away from the food and the hoopla of nations,
let myself be led to the still lines
waiting in the August heat.
I felt the cold presence of the building
as we entered and stepped on the moving belt.

Floating slowly on our dark way,
I thought how the statue was always noise
until the chisel's final glancing,

how quiet suddenly filled his room
with completion designed to last
in a world I could not imagine.
But Michelangelo Buonarroti, knowing
things are always waiting to emerge,
might well understand the conveyor
sliding us from sunlight to sunlight
on seven minutes of night—a chip of silence
gathered from Gotham's astounding mass.
He might accept the great glass wall
rising to hold back everything,
including the bullets he had never seen.
He might even sense this belt and window
to have grown from the statue itself:
the swell of completion and isolation
loosed by his own hands,
the *noli me tangere* feeding our awe.

3. The Schooling of Lazlo Toth
Layers were always his life.
His mother buried him with blankets
so that dark became heat and weight,
then sang and peeled them one by one,
calling him back to her face and light—
his small back arching from the bed
in a child's hope of levitation,
knowing how in seconds he'd be free.

For Hungarian winter she wrapped him:
stockings and socks and woolens,
shirts and sweaters and coats.
Out through the icy streets and back,
gently stripped at her hands before the fire—
his body emerging from its mummied stance,
warmer and warmer the less it wore.
On one walk he fell and was bruised
even through the clothing's cushion.

The rock-point's damage hurt him more
with every garment she lifted off,
as if the wound were really growing
from her hands. But when it lay revealed,
a dull red shine like the stove's,
her hands were the only comfort.

The great gash of cliff above their town:
picnics at its base, climbs to the top
through the grassy slopes behind the face.
His father always pointing out the crush
laid by time on rock, the dull and shimmering veins;
his notion born for giving life to stone
by learning to speak its names and depths.
Tied by ropes to the roots above
they'd edge down fissures
until from the top they looked,
Mother said, like heads resting on the grass.
Then farther down, Father saying stretch
your fingers wide and lay them flat
and touch more years than Man has walked the earth.

4. *Nineteenth Century: The Priests Improve the Statue*

If the shepherds stray, shall the sheep be blamed for straying likewise?

Hail Mary, full of grace and brackets . . .

In the hearts of the holy fathers
the need for haloes was discerned
and the means discovered: Christ the tricky
job with his head supine, drilled
through the top and plugged with a rod,
the shining metal circle affixed.
Mary with clamps at her nape—
the cliffs of Carrara moaning in the wind,
the haloes pulsing sickly light
for the eyes of the blind.

5. The Song of Lazlo Toth
It was Her. Him I would not touch,
the One who suffered, who was dead and sagged
on that hand that had never not touched Him.
But Her. That face so at ease, so glib,
bowed as if thinking of a story
She'd heard, and trying to be sad.
Never hungry in Her life, never alone.
I went for the eyes. You've seen them?
Up close? Beneath those lids—nothing!

The stone cried for release, and I came.
The papers say fifteen times, or eleven.
It was again and again, and never enough.
Her arm hitting the floor was beauty itself.

My mother starved while guards were paid
to strut St. Peter's for the sake of rock.
Buonarroti, your hands are dust.
If I had found that slab on the beach,
so oddly shaped by the tumblings of God,
I'd have heaved it straight back to the sea.

6. Photographer
She was a new shot each time that he swung:
small pocks like craters opening,
one by one, in the softness of stone;
her arm at the instant it fell.
I never thought to look away
or run him down, took my eye
from the zoom lens only once—
discovered then the scene's failure,
the loss of tight detail.

Soon she would be coddled, remade
in her own image, glorious
fake that her maker alone might detect.

Only at first was she mine: my shutters
opened her far beyond
any vision that Joseph had known.

7. Souvenir Hunter's Prayer
The hole in my hand
throbs and exists
in my thoughts alone—
those fearing storms
need no storms to fear.
I know what I have—
body of God's mother—
and where it belongs.
I watched them all on their knees
on ladders the following day:
picking through the piled-up wax
crusting the holders and walls,
dreamers on a fantastic dig.

Define a true relic?
One that cannot be held.
Returning to the Dome,
approaching the curate,
I'll grope for the right word:
Shard. Fragment. Chip. Fleck.
Let him deal with it—
glue it back, toss it away.
At least I know my meanings
when they have burned me.
May all others learn
this much. Amen.

8. The Restorers' Debate

     i
Truest creation obliges us all
to enter the world it has made. Come hell
or high water, heaven or searing drought,

we must acknowledge the power of heart
crossed with starred hands and gifted intellect:
such sacred projects are forever flecked
golden by special light, never to be
destroyed or stolen, never to be
equalled in their spirits or their honed skills.
But what they are, they *must* remain through time:
we have the means to save appearances,
must dutifully reclaim originals
from accidents, war, and weather—from slime
walking in human form, doing the devil's dance.

ii

Just to feel her this way is far too much,
running my fingers over the hard stump
left below her shoulder, forcing my touch
on the shattered nose's triangular hump—
all this in the name of gaining some sense
for matching up these grainy surfaces
with the chunks and splinters I'll dandle next,
as if such art could be jigsaw pieces.
To repair her would imply that she *works*
like some engine or ceramic jug,
and that she was merely *made* for our gawks,
anonymous plaster donkey or dog.
The artist's sacred circle shelters all—
creates the rise, encompasses the fall.

9. Lurleen Wallace Considers the News at Her Sleeping Husband's Bedside
So here is what another six days can make:
George with a promise of life, though frozen forever—
that bastard Bremer's bullet a nail
driving our spines to a clicking and humming chair.
And now this statue, shattered and cried for everywhere,
shrouded and placed in the hands of restorers
whose money and months will give her perfection again.
Arthur Bremer. Lazlo Toth. How many names for hate!

George, this commentator speaks of art and life,
says that many will weep for rock yet not for you,
says there are things that cannot be replaced
and things that cannot be replaced.
George, I wish I didn't want to read this,
wish I didn't have these photos of the whole and broken.
He says, "Forgive me, please, but money makes the world—
her art, her politics and sex—go 'round."
He says the Vatican invested wealth in art
believing in a visual ride to heaven,
says we tried the identical trip
on the sweating backs of slaves.
Says every assassin has been poor, or afraid of poverty.

Christ, George, what does anyone know
unless he's lived at the center and on top at once?
Remember how you told me we could rise and rise,
carrying the righteous with us
while the empty fell away below?
I swear I don't know anything, except
the world is what those who make it make it.
Yes, I'll run for governor—
me your back and you my tongue,
holding each other up as we must.

10. Pietà: For My Father
This will not be easy, this denouncing.

So much of what he felt was always right
in that second, midnight world
where accountant would be architect—
the ciphers and terms of analysis raised
to envisioning forms in space,
to clothing the air itself.

• • •

Sketching on the backs of his ledger sheets
the vaultings of buildings or a vibrating pillow
to waken the hard of hearing,

my father had dreams of invention and craft.
Just married, he stood at the white mountain
raised by a snow-covered stockpile of coal,
and there—as my mother sat miles away,
darning socks while chicken baked in the cramped kitchen—
he learned the bounds of imagination
for junior accountants on inventory jobs:
pacing off and sighting up the hill,
poking the depths of snow with sticks,
concocting his own equations and stats,
he managed a figure too clear and close
for the day's adverse conditions;
juggling his own numbers to back off from truth,
he was hailed for exacting work.

      • • •

In the shadowed light of that moon called *blue*
we may rise to occasional wisdom.
That one morning in 1972,
above the rounds of muffins and eggs
I raised my section of the paper to counter his.
We had always been a cartoon breakfast—
my father an expanse of newsprint
fringed by sets of fingers and wreathed by smoke,
mother the quiet shuffler, cooking and pouring.
Growing up, I had envied the great
Italian families in movies, yakking and laughing
across a long, massive table,
inventing their days at breakfast
and recounting them there at night.
But silence was our usual word,
even in those later years
when I came to table as visitor,
sprawling my legs in the space beneath—
the open shell of a family grown.

That one day in 1972,
the rare cry of print
only the avid can hear as they read:

the Blessed Virgin pummeled and split—
not in her spirit, for which I had no use,
but in her body of art, irreplaceable.
Across the table, I counted
on my father's second self to rise to my call,
but he shrugged aside my sorrow
at the fury of Lazlo Toth,
turned again to the things of his world.

> • • •

My loss was not the indifference
but the fragile void of its causes,
the way a life we love can be steered,
beyond our control, beyond us.
I thought how stately and sprawling old homes in the country,
accosted now by highways jammed up to their porches,
surely must be among the saddest things on earth.
They are what they were yet are utterly changed,
webbed in the world that made them,
nothing but all that they have to be.

If one needs all his life
to write each poem, this only says
his entire life is what he needs
for anything he'll ever say or do.
We wear the past like leaded boots
on astronauts who walk the moon—
the heavy exertion of every step
our only chance to keep from drifting off.

Alfred Corn

Sugar Cane

> Some view our sable race with scornful eye,
> "Their color is a diabolic dye."
> Remember, Christians, Negroes, black as Cain,
> May be refined, and join the angelic train.
> —Phillis Wheatley, "On Being Brought
>   from Africa to America"

The mother bending over a baby named Shug
chuckles, "Gimme some sugar," just to preface
a flurry of kisses sweet as sugar cane.
Later, when she stirs a spoonful of Domino
into her coffee, who's to tell the story
how a ten-foot-tall reed from the Old World,
on being brought to the New, was raised and cropped
so cooks could sweeten whatever tasted bitter?
Or how grade-A granulated began as a thick
black syrup boiled for hours in an iron vat
until it was refined to pure, white crystal.

When I was a child whose payoff for obeying
orders was red-and-white-striped candy canes,
I knew that sugar was love.
The first time someone called me "sweetheart,"
I knew sugar was love.
And when I tasted my slice of the wedding cake,
iced white and washed down with sweet champagne,
don't you know sugar was love.

One day Evelina who worked for us
showed up with her son Bubba and laughed,

"Now y'all can play together." He had a sweet
nature, but even so we raised a little Cain,
and Daddy told her not to bring him back.
He thought I'd begun to sound like colored people.
She smiled, dropped her eyes, kept working.
And kept putting on weight. She later died of stroke.
Daddy developed diabetes by age fifty-five,
insulin burned what his blood couldn't handle.
Chronic depressions I have, a nutritionist
gently termed "the sugar blues," but damned
if any lyrics came out of them, baby.

Black-and-white negatives from a picture
history of the sugar trade develop
in my dreams, a dozen able-bodied slaves
hacking forward through a field of cane.
Sweat trickles down from forehead into eye
as they sheave up stalks and cart them to the mill
where grinding iron rollers will express a thin
sucrose solution that, when not refined,
goes from blackstrap molasses on into rum,
a demon conveniently negotiable for slaves.
The master under the impression he owned
these useful properties naturally never thought
of offering *them* a piece of the wedding cake,
the big white house that bubbling brown sugar built
and paid for, unnaturally processed by Domino.

Phyllis Wheatley said the sweet Christ was brought
here from Asia Minor to redeem an African child
and maybe her master's soul as well. She wrote
as she lived, a model of refinement, yes,
but black as Abel racing through the canebrake,
demon bloodhounds baying in pursuit,
until at last his brother caught him,
expressed his rage, and rode back home to dinner.
Tell it to Fats Domino, to those who live

on Sugar Hill, tell it to unsuspecting Shug
as soon as she is old enough to hear it.

One day Evelina's son waved goodbye
and climbed on board a northbound train,
black angels guiding him invisibly.
In class he quoted a sentence from Jean Toomer:
"Time and space have no meaning in a canefield."

My father died last fall at eighty-one.
Love's bitter, child, as often as it's sweet.
Mm-mm, I sure do have the blues today:
Baby, will you give me some sugar?

After Neruda

His clothes stripped off the fisherman raises his spear
stalking the trapped fish that circles a rock pool
Sea   air   and man all stand motionless
Compassion like a rose maybe blossoms
at the water's edge and slowly rises
soothing the jagged moment with calm
One by one each minute seems to close
on its elder like folds in a fan
Then the naked fisherman's heart
appeased its pounding in the sea
and when the rocks were not watching
and while the wave unraveled its strength
straight to the core of that speechless world
he let fire a lightning bolt
against the still life of the stone
The spear plunged into brute matter
The struck fish throbbed rising to light
cruel flag on an impassive sea
butterfly of blood-streaked salt

The Shouters

A fiercer form of homelessness, an exile
From the brisk release that conversation offers:
You've heard them on the street, snapped to alert
As they barked cusswords at—what? some blood-red
Ghost that loomed and stalked as you approached.

That sweeping hand, as though it held a gavel,
Flung down a tattered gauntlet or was aiming
Karate chops at an invisible
Assailant, adds the punch of blunt conviction
To words that pump white steam into the cold.

Common explanations, whether hormonal
Failure (aging women diagnostic
Victims of that), schizophrenia, booze,
Downtown attitude or bigotry,
Don't quite account for voices raw as theirs.

What makes you stop and see this one as crowned
With a halo of syringes, each injecting
Various doses of addictive damage
Since childhood, when a parent screamed "Shut up,"
Or the year love crashed down around his head, or—

"Shut *up!*" he shouts (as others have) and shudders
Enough to block overtures always worth
Risking . . . unless it's clear a mind divided
Is getting back at itself and will go on
To heights where the air burns thin and it can shout
And shout until encroaching silence falls—
Sheltered up there, where all our cries are heard.

Rosemary Daniell

Of Jayne Mansfield, Flannery O'Connor, My Mother & Me

for Alice Walker, whose blackness made the enemy visible

Myth of the Spanish moss:
within each hard tree   a bound
woman writhes: her hair   twists
of ash   claws crawls the air. . . .
in Milledgeville   live oaks
blanch the Blood of the Lambs—
debs in white cotton panties
crimped matrons in slips of white
lace   all the permanent Daughters
of the Confederacy   caught
in their corsets of white
brocade.   Yes   this is an ash
blonde town   the white satin
undergarment of the Baptist
Belt   of swamps where white
crewcut sheriffs run down blacks
& women.   It's three A.M.

& I lie in the John Milledge
Motel   room 4D   where Jayne
Mansfield slept   a half-mile
down Highway 441
from the white town house where
Flannery stitched the white
home ec apron required for her
graduation from the same
school where my mother wore

white middy blouses   wrote on
white notebook paper   "I want
to marry a lawyer   live in
a house with white columns. . . ."

& trying not to hear   through
white walls the sounds of white
male cursing   I think Jayne
her white satin hair spreading
her white plastic breasts rising
beneath this cover of white
chenille   the white white sperm
of half of Amerika   gliding
across her light pancaked cheeks—
& imagine Flannery   sweet
between her white girl's sheets
watching upon a white white
ceiling   blank white pages
the petits fours with white icing
of literary teas   & now flash
my mother   her Pond's palms
pressed against her   magnolia
petal face   dreaming the blonde
man who would save her   the white
white roses   the white satin
wedding   the honeymoon trip.

Yet listening to the *mother*
fuckers   sons of bitches
the brute motel plans made by
white southern men   I wonder:
did Jayne see already   her
decapitation on a dark road
outside New Orleans   her head
that Clairol-pale egg   severed
as in life from her body?
Or did Flannery   Catholic &

weird   feel even then the wolf
disease   eating out her teen
age limbs: the falling hair
melting hipbones   the hospital
cuff   tightening   tightening?

& did my mother   even before
my Cherokee-tinged father—
the drinking & the gambling—
the bills & torn underwear—
sob into her dormitory
pillow   bubbling within her
belle's brainpan with the
lobotomies of marriage
the electrodes for shock   her
suicide at sixty?   Yes

did each of them: Jayne
her throat neatly stitched
Flannery   her face turned
moony by cortisone   my mother
whitened to wax by Revlon
her upper lip bleached blonde
wearing her best white gold
costume jewelry   yes   did
each of them know   lying
in this white satin–lined
sarcophagus for women   that
the first drop of blood ruins
the crotches of white cotton
panties   spots the slips of
white nylon lace   stains the backs
of white wedding dresses   yes
turns each of us scarlet women
deserving of mutilation
disease   damnation   that we
like the women in the trees

are embalmed   & recalling
my rage   washing between pale
blue lines   the blood-black scrawl
of my mother's girlish plans
I wonder what sleep awaits me—
freak of cunt & brain   in this
place   pure   white   chaste

The Distant War

Outside Atlanta, 1967

At the kitchen sink
you cut   through
a bunch of lettuce.
Your hand pushing leaves
you dream the brush of jungle:
greener   rough & stinging:
through the plumpness of your thigh
a sear runs like shrapnel

& you recall   how
at noon   women at the luncheon
ate Baked Alaska:
jeweled fingers moved spoons
toward mouths that
between bits of dripping sugar
dropped words like:
"War should be declared."

& a woman in a flowered hat
as wide as she
had a balloon from her mouth
that said
"Those men are not our kind . . .
we must protect our own ways. . . ."

like luncheons   like Baked Alaskas
like spoons & jeweled fingers.
Yet to you   in your kitchen
expansions of spices
rise to contain a sting:
loosed in the cut on your thumb
does the vinegar for salad burn
more than the metal that pours
through a boy's thigh through way of yours:
a burning he can't tear out of his skin
a burning you soon cannot tear out of yours

as you place the salad inside the bowl
as over coffee   you sit & read:
you   the well-read housewife reads:
on arts *The Village Voice* states:
   Marc Morrell makes forms out of flags
   Marc Morrell stuffs the flag and chokes it with a rope
   Marc Morrell is charged   the gallery owner is charged
   perjury on those dead pieces of cloth
cotton is the dead flower of the cotton plant
the flag was made from cotton
killed   colored   dyed

ripped from their bolls
like leaves of lettuce
are ripped from their core

like boys are ripped from their lives.

& preparing the flesh
of a lamb for broiling
you watch interviews
on television: homefront opinions:
in a party hat of tinfoil
a patron of the local VFW states
"The killing of women and children is just a natural part of it"

of war
our natural occupation
of war
our mass death wish
of war
thousands upon thousands of homosexual grapplings

Yet this moment   on your kitchen stool
sits your neighbor's son   not yet twenty
come to say good-bye   he tells you
he is not afraid   only of not being brave if captured
"My friend, you would not tell with such high zest
To children ardent for some desperate glory,
The old lie: *Dulce et decorum est*
Pro patria mori."

But your neighbor's son
hasn't read Wilfred Owen
& if he did   wouldn't believe it—
he only sits & talks
of guns   of mud   of the girls of Saigon

& you   listening
hear only his scream   noting
the hairs on his arm are as light as your baby's
the muscles lumps of semiprecious substance
to be kept from jungle sun and melting.
To be kept from hot places like wars.

James Dickey

The Lifeguard

In a stable of boats I lie still,
From all sleeping children hidden.
The leap of a fish from its shadow
Makes the whole lake instantly tremble.
With my foot on the water, I feel
The moon outside

Take on the utmost of its power.
I rise and go out through the boats.
I set my broad sole upon silver,
On the skin of the sky, on the moonlight,
Stepping outward from earth onto water
In quest of the miracle

This village of children believed
That I could perform as I dived
For one who had sunk from my sight.
I saw his cropped haircut go under.
I leapt, and my steep body flashed
Once, in the sun.

Dark drew all light from my eyes.
Like a man who explores his death
By the pull of his slow-moving shoulders,
I hung head down in the cold,
Wide-eyed, contained, and alone
Among the weeds,

And my fingertips turned into stone
From clutching immovable blackness.
Time after time I leapt upward
Exploding in breath, and fell back
From the change in the children's faces
At my defeat.

Beneath them I swam to the boathouse
With only my life in my arms
To wait for the lake to shine back
At the risen moon with such power
That my steps on the light of the ripples
Might be sustained.

Beneath me is nothing but brightness
Like the ghost of a snowfield in summer.
As I move toward the center of the lake,
Which is also the center of the moon,
I am thinking of how I may be
The savior of one

Who has already died in my care.
The dark trees fade from around me.
The moon's dust hovers together.
I call softly out, and the child's
Voice answers through blinding water.
Patiently, slowly,

He rises, dilating to break
The surface of stone with his forehead.
He is one I do not remember
Having ever seen in his life.
The ground I stand on is trembling
Upon his smile.

I wash the black mud from my hands.
On a light given off by the grave

I kneel in the quick of the moon
At the heart of a distant forest
And hold in my arms a child
Of water, water, water.

In the Mountain Tent

I am hearing the shape of the rain
Take the shape of the tent and believe it,
Laying down all around where I lie
A profound, unspeakable law.
I obey, and am free-falling slowly

Through the thought-out leaves of the wood
Into the minds of animals.
I am there in the shining of water
Like dark, like light, out of Heaven.

I am there like the dead, or the beast
Itself, which thinks of a poem—
Green, plausible, living, and holy—
And cannot speak, but hears,
Called forth from the waiting of things,

A vast, proper, reinforced crying
With the sifted, harmonious pause,
The sustained intake of all breath
Before the first word of the Bible.

At midnight water dawns
Upon the held skulls of the foxes
And weasels and tousled hares
On the eastern side of the mountain.
Their light is the image I make

As I wait as if recently killed,
Receptive, fragile, half-smiling,
My brow watermarked with the mark
On the wing of a moth

And the tent taking shape on my body
Like ill-fitting, Heavenly clothes.
From holes in the ground comes my voice
In the God-silenced tongue of the beasts.
"I shall rise from the dead," I am saying.

Cherrylog Road

Off Highway 106
At Cherrylog Road I entered
The '34 Ford without wheels,
Smothered in kudzu,
With a seat pulled out to run
Corn whiskey from the hills,

And then from the other side
Crept into an Essex
With a rumble seat of red leather
And then out again, aboard
A blue Chevrolet, releasing
The rust from its other color,

Reared up on three building blocks.
None had the same body heat;
I changed with them inward, toward
The weedy heart of the junkyard,
For I knew that Doris Holbrook
Would escape from her father at noon

And would come from the farm
To seek parts owned by the sun

Among the abandoned chassis,
Sitting in each in turn
As I did, leaning forward
As in a wild stock-car race

In the parking lot of the dead.
Time after time, I climbed in
And out the other side, like
An envoy or movie star
Met at the station by crickets.
A radiator cap raised its head,

Became a real toad or a kingsnake
As I neared the hub of the yard,
Passing through many states,
Many lives, to reach
Some grandmother's long Pierce-Arrow
Sending platters of blindness forth

From its nickel hubcaps
And spilling its tender upholstery
On sleepy roaches,
The glass panel in between
Lady and colored driver
Not all the way broken out,

The back-seat phone
Still on its hook.
I got in as though to exclaim,
"Let us go to the orphan asylum,
John; I have some old toys
For children who say their prayers."

I popped with sweat as I thought
I heard Doris Holbrook scrape
Like a mouse in the southern-state sun
That was eating the paint in blisters

From a hundred car tops and hoods.
She was tapping like code,

Loosening the screws,
Carrying off headlights,
Sparkplugs, bumpers,
Cracked mirrors and gear-knobs,
Getting ready, already,
To go back with something to show

Other than her lips' new trembling
I would hold to me soon, soon,
Where I sat in the ripped back seat
Talking over the interphone,
Praying for Doris Holbrook
To come from her father's farm

And to get back there
With no trace of me on her face
To be seen by her red-haired father
Who would change, in the squalling barn,
Her back's pale skin with a strop,
Then lay for me

In a bootlegger's roasting car
With a string-triggered 12-gauge shotgun
To blast the breath from the air.
Not cut by the jagged windshields,
Through the acres of wrecks she came
With a wrench in her hand,

Through dust where the blacksnake dies
Of boredom, and the beetle knows
The compost has no more life.
Someone outside would have seen
The oldest car's door inexplicably
Close from within:

I held her and held her and held her,
Convoyed at terrific speed
By the stalled, dreaming traffic around us,
So the blacksnake, stiff
With inaction, curved back
Into life, and hunted the mouse

With deadly overexcitement,
The beetles reclaimed their field
As we clung, glued together,
With the hooks of the seat springs
Working through to catch us red-handed
Amidst the gray breathless batting

That burst from the seat at our backs.
We left by separate doors
Into the changed, other bodies
Of cars, she down Cherrylog Road
And I to my motorcycle
Parked like the soul of the junkyard

Restored, a bicycle fleshed
With power, and tore off
Up Highway 106, continually
Drunk on the wind in my mouth,
Wringing the handlebar for speed,
Wild to be wreckage forever.

Drinking from a Helmet

I
I climbed out, tired of waiting
For my foxhole to turn in the earth
On its side or its back for a grave,
And got in line

Somewhere in the roaring of dust.
Every tree on the island was nowhere,
Blasted away.

II
In the middle of combat, a graveyard
Was advancing after the troops
With laths and balls of string;
Grass already tinged it with order.
Between the new graves and the foxholes
A green water-truck stalled out.
I moved up on it, behind
The hill that cut off the firing.

III
My turn, and I shoved forward
A helmet I picked from the ground,
Not daring to take mine off
Where somebody else may have come
Loose from the steel of his head.

IV
Keeping the foxhole doubled
In my body and begging
For water, safety, and air,
I drew water out of the truckside
As if dreaming the helmet full.
In my hands, the sun
Came on in a feathery light.

V
In midair, water trimming
To my skinny dog-faced look
Showed my life's first all-out beard
Growing wildly, escaping from childhood,
Like the beards of the dead, all now
Underfoot beginning to grow.

Selected ripples wove through it,
Knocked loose with a touch from all sides
Of a brain killed early that morning,
Most likely, and now
In its absence holding
My sealed, sunny image from harm,
Weighing down my hands,
Shipping at the edges,
Too heavy on one side, then the other.

VI
I drank, with the timing of rust.
A vast military wedding
Somewhere advanced one step.

VII
All around, equipment drifting in light,
Men drinking like cattle and bushes,
Cans, leather, canvas and rifles,
Grass pouring down from the sun
And up from the ground.
Grass: and the summer advances
Invisibly into the tropics.
Wind, and the summer shivers
Through many men standing or lying
In the GI gardener's hand
Spreading and turning green
All over the hill.

VIII
At the middle of water
Bright circles dawned inward and outward
Like oak rings surviving the tree
As its soul, or like
The concentric gold spirit of time.
I kept trembling forward through something
Just born of me.

IX

My nearly dead power to pray
Like an army increased and assembled,
As when, in a harvest of sparks,
The helmet leapt from the furnace
And clamped itself
On the heads of a billion men.
Some words directed to Heaven
Went through all the strings of the graveyard
Like a message that someone sneaked in,
Tapping a telegraph key
At dead of night, then running
For his life.

X

I swayed, as if kissed in the brain.
Above the shelled palm-stumps I saw
How the tops of huge trees might be moved
In a place in my own country
I never had seen in my life.
In the closed dazzle of my mouth
I fought with a word in the water
To call on the dead to strain
Their muscles to get up and go there.
I felt the difference between
Sweat and tears when they rise,
Both trying to melt the brow down.

XI

On even the first day of death
The dead cannot rise up,
But their last thought hovers somewhere
For whoever finds it.
My uninjured face floated strangely
In the rings of a bodiless tree.
Among them, also, a final
Idea lived, waiting
As in Ariel's limbed, growing jail.

XII
I stood as though I possessed
A cool, trembling man
Exactly my size, swallowed whole.
Leather swung at his waist,
Web-cord, buckles, and metal,
Crouching over the dead
Where they waited for all their hands
To be connected like grass-roots.

XIII
In the brown half-life of my beard
The hair stood up
Like the awed hair lifting the back
Of a dog that has eaten a swan.
Now light like this
Staring into my face
Was the first thing around me at birth.
Be no more killed, it said.

XIV
The wind in the grass
Moved gently in secret flocks,
Then spread to be
Nothing, just where they were.
In delight's
Whole shining condition and risk,
I could see how my body might come
To be imagined by something
That thought of it only for joy.

XV
Fresh sweat and unbearable tears
Drawn up by my feet from the field
Between my eyebrows became
One thing at last,
And I could cry without hiding.
The world dissolved into gold;

I could have stepped up into air.
I drank and finished
Like tasting of Heaven,
Which is simply of,
At seventeen years,
Not dying wherever you are.

XVI
Enough
Shining, I picked up my carbine and said.
I threw my old helmet down
And put the wet one on.
Warmed water ran over my face.
My last thought changed, and I knew
I inherited one of the dead.

XVII
I saw tremendous trees
That would grow on the sun if they could,
Towering. I saw a fence
and two boys facing each other,
Quietly talking,
Looking in at the gigantic redwoods,
The rings in the trunks turning slowly
To raise up stupendous green.
They went away, one turning
The wheels of a blue bicycle,
The smaller one curled catercornered
In the handlebar basket.

XVIII
I would survive and go there,
Stepping off the train in a helmet
That held a man's last thought,
Which showed him his older brother
Showing him trees.
I would ride through all

California upon two wheels
Until I came to the white
Dirt road where they had been,
Hoping to meet his blond brother,
And to walk with him into the wood
Until we were lost,
Then take off the helmet
And tell him where I had stood,
What poured, what spilled, what swallowed:

XIX
And tell him I was the man.

Pursuit from Under

Often, in these blue meadows,
I hear what passes for the bark of seals

And on August week ends the cold of a personal ice age
Comes up through my bare feet
Which are trying to walk like a boy's again
So that nothing on earth can have changed
On the ground where I was raised.

The dark grass here is like
The pads of mukluks going on and on

Because I once burned kerosene to read
Myself near the North Pole
In the journal of Arctic explorers
Found, years after death, preserved
In a tent, part of whose canvas they had eaten

Before the last entry.
All over my father's land

The seal holes sigh like an organ,
And one entry carries more terror
Than the blank page that signified death
In 1912, on the icecap.
It says that, under the ice,

The killer whale darts and distorts,
Cut down by the flawing glass

To a weasel's shadow,
And when, through his ceiling, he sees
Anything darker than snow
He falls away
To gather more and more force

From the iron depths of cold water,
His shadow dwindling

Almost to nothing at all, then charges
Straight up, looms up at the ice and smashes
Into it with his forehead
To splinter the roof, to isolate seal or man
On a drifting piece of the floe

Which he can overturn.
If you run, he will follow you

Under the frozen pane,
Turning as you do, zigzagging,
And at the most uncertain of your ground
Will shatter through, and lean,
And breathe frankly in your face

An enormous breath smelling of fish.
With the stale lungs staining your air

You know the unsaid recognition
Of which the explorers died:

They had been given an image
Of how the downed dead pursue us.
They knew, as they starved to death,

That not only in the snow
But in the family field

The small shadow moves,
And under bare feet in the summer:
That somewhere the turf will heave,
And the outraged breath of the dead,
So long held, will form

Unbreathably around the living.
The cows low oddly here

As I pass, a small bidden shape
Going with me, trembling like foxfire
Under my heels and their hooves.
I shall write this by kerosene,
Pitch a tent in the pasture, and starve.

Looking for the Buckhead Boys

Some of the time, going home, I go
Blind and can't find it.
The house I lived in growing up and out
The doors of high school is torn
Down and cleared
Away for further development, but that does not stop me.
First in the heart
Of my blind spot are
The Buckhead Boys. If I can find them, even one,
I'm home. And if I can find him catch him in or around
Buckhead, I'll never die; it's likely my youth will walk
Inside me like a king.

First of all, going home, I must go
To Wender and Roberts' Drug Store, for driving through I saw it
Shining   renewed   renewed
In chromium, but still there.
It's one of the places the Buckhead Boys used to be, before
Beer turned teen-ager.
                                                    Tommy Nichols
Is not there. The Drug Store is full of women
Made of cosmetics. Tommy Nichols has never been
In such a place: he was the Number Two Man on the Mile
Relay Team in his day.
                                                    What day?
My day. Where was I?
                        Number Three, and there are some sunlit pictures
In the Book of the Dead to prove it: the 1939
North Fulton High School Annual. Go down,
                        Go down

                To Tyree's Pool Hall, for there was more
                        Concentration of the spirit
                        Of the Buckhead Boys
In there, than anywhere else in the world.
                                                    Do I want some shoes
                To walk all over Buckhead like a king
                Nobody knows? Well, I can get them at Tyree's;
        It's a shoe store now. I could tell you where every spittoon
Ought to be standing. Charlie Gates used to say one of these days
                I'm gonna get myself the reputation of being
        The bravest man in Buckhead. I'm going in Tyree's toilet
        And pull down my pants and take a shit.
                                                    Maybe
Charlie's the key: the man who would say that would never leave
Buckhead. Where is he? Maybe I ought to look up
        Some Old Merchants. Why didn't I think of that
        Before?
                Lord, Lord! Like a king!

Hardware. Hardware and Hardware Merchants
Never die, and they have everything on hand
There is to know. Somewhere in the wood-screws Mr. Hamby may have
My Prodigal's Crown on sale. He showed up
For every football game at home
Or away, in the hills of North Georgia. There he is, as old
As ever.
Mr. Hamby, remember me?
God A'Mighty! Ain't you the one
Who fumbled the punt and lost the Russell game?
That's right.
How're them butter fingers?
Still butter, I say,
Still fumbling, But what about the rest of the team? What about Charlie
Gates?
He the boy that got lime in his eye from the goal line
When y'all played Gainesville?
Right.
I don't know. Seems to me I see . . .

See? See? What does Charlie Gates see in his eye burning
With the goal line? Does he see a middle-aged man from the Book
Of the Dead looking for him in magic shoes
From Tyree's disappeared pool hall?
Mr. Hamby, Mr. Hamby,
Where? Where is Mont Black?
Paralyzed. Doctors can't do nothing.
Where is Dick Shea?
Assistant Sales Manager
Of Kraft Cheese.
How about Punchy Henderson?
Died of a heart attack
Watching high school football
In South Carolina.
Old Punchy, the last
Of the windsprinters, and now for no reason the first
Of the heart attacks.

Looking for the Buckhead Boys   97

Harmon Quigley?

He's up at County Work Farm

Sixteen. Doing all right up there; be out next year.

Didn't anybody get to be a doctor?

Or lawyer?

Sure. Bobby Laster's a chiropractor. He's right out here

At Bolton; got a real good business.

Jack Siple?

Moved away.

Gordon Hamm?

Dead

In the war.

O the Book

Of the Dead, and the dead bright sun on the page

Where the team stands ready to explode

In all directions with Time. Did you say you see Charlie

Gates every now and then?

Seems to me.

Where?

He may be out yonder at the Gulf Station between here and Sandy

Springs

Let me go pull my car out

Of the parking lot in back

Of Wender and Roberts'. Do I need gas? No; let me drive around the block

Let me drive around Buckhead

A few dozen times   turning   turning in my foreign

Car till the town spins   whirls till the chrome vanishes

From Wender and Roberts'   the spittoons are remade

From the sun itself   the dead pages flutter the hearts rise up, that lie

In the ground, and Bobby Laster's backbreaking fingers

Pick up a cue-stick   Tommy Nichols and I rack the balls

And Charlie Gates walks into Tyree's un-

imaginable toilet.

I go north

Now, and I can use fifty

Cents' worth of gas.

It is Gulf. I pull in and praise the Lord Charlie
Gates comes out. His blue shirt dazzles
Like a baton-pass. He squints he looks at me
Through the goal line. Charlie, Charlie, we have won away from
We have won at home
In the last minute. Can you see me? You say
What I say: where in God
Almighty have you been all this time? I don't know,
Charlie. I don't know. But I've come to tell you a secret
That has to be put into code. Understand what I mean when I say
To the one man who came back alive
From the Book of the Dead   to the bravest man
In Buckhead   to the lime-eyed ghost
Blue-wavering in the fumes
Of good Gulf gas, "Fill 'er up."
With wine? Light? Heart-attack blood? The contents of Tyree's toilet? The beer
Of teen-age sons? No; just
"Fill 'er up. Fill 'er up, Charlie."

For the Last Wolverine

They will soon be down

To one, but he still will be
For a little while   still will be stopping

The flakes in the air with a look,
Surrounding himself with the silence
Of whitening snarls. Let him eat
The last red meal of the condemned

To extinction, tearing the guts

From an elk. Yet that is not enough
For me. I would have him eat

The heart, and, from it, have an idea
Stream into his gnawing head
That he no longer has a thing
To lose, and so can walk

Out into the open, in the full

Pale of the sub-Arctic sun
Where a single spruce tree is dying

Higher and higher. Let him climb it
With all his meanness and strength.
Lord, we have come to the end
Of this kind of vision of heaven,

As the sky breaks open

Its fans around him and shimmers
And into its northern gates he rises

Snarling   complete   in the joy of a weasel
With an elk's horned heart in his stomach
Looking straight into the eternal
Blue, where he hauls his kind. I would have it all

My way: at the top of that tree I place

The New World's last eagle
Hunched in mangy feathers   giving

Up on the theory of flight.
Dear God of the wildness of poetry, let them mate
To the death in the rotten branches,
Let the tree sway and burst into flame

And mingle them, crackling with feathers,

In crownfire. Let something come
Of it   something gigantic   legendary

Rise beyond reason over hills
Of ice   SCREAMING   that it cannot die,
That it has come back, this time
On wings, and will spare no earthly thing:

That it will hover, made purely of northern

Lights, at dusk   and fall
On men building roads: will perch

On the moose's horn like a falcon
Riding into battle   into holy war against
Screaming railroad crews: will pull
Whole traplines like fibres from the snow

In the long-jawed night of fur trappers.

But, small, filthy, unwinged,
You will soon be crouching

Alone, with maybe some dim racial notion
Of being the last, but none of how much
Your unnoticed going will mean:
How much the timid poem needs

The mindless explosion of your rage,

The glutton's internal fire   the elk's
Heart in the belly, sprouting wings,

The pact of the "blind swallowing
Thing," with himself, to eat
The world, and not to be driven off it
Until it is gone, even if it takes

Forever. I take you as you are

And make of you what I will,
Skunk-bear, carcajou, bloodthirsty

Non-survivor.
                        Lord, let me die   but not die
Out.

W. E. B. Du Bois

The Song of the Smoke

>   I am the Smoke King
>   I am black!
> I am swinging in the sky,
> I am wringing worlds awry;
> I am the thought of the throbbing mills,
> I am the soul of the soul-toil kills,
> Wraith of the ripple of trading rills;
> Up I'm curling from the sod,
> I am whirling home to God;
>   I am the Smoke King
>   I am black.
>
>   I am the Smoke King,
>   I am black!
> I am wreathing broken hearts,
> I am sheathing love's light darts;
>   Inspiration of iron times
>   Wedding the toil of toiling climes,
>   Shedding the blood of bloodless crimes—
> Lurid lowering 'mid the blue
> Torrid towering toward the true,
>   I am the Smoke King,
>   I am black.
>
>   I am the Smoke King,
>   I am black!
> I am darkening with song,
> I am harkening to wrong!
>   I will be black as blackness can—

The blacker the mantle, the mightier the man!
For blackness was ancient ere whiteness began.
I am daubing God in night,
I am swabbing Hell in white:
   I am the Smoke King
   I am black.

   I am the Smoke King
   I am black!
I am cursing ruddy morn,
I am hearsing hearts unborn:
   Souls unto me are as stars in a night,
   I whiten my black men—I blacken my white!
   What's the hue of a hide to a man in his might?
Hail! great, gritty, grimy hands—
Sweet Christ, pity toiling lands!
   I am the Smoke King
   I am black.

The Song of America

I doom, I live, I will,
I take, I lie, I kill!
I rend and rear
In deserts drear—
I build and burrow well.
With wrack and rue
I hound and hew
On founding stones in Hell:
My Temples rise
And split the Skies,
My winged wheels do tell
The woven wonders of my hand,
The witch-work of my skill!
I writhe, I rave,

I chain the Slave
I do the deed, I kill!
Now what care I
For God or Lie?
I am the great
I WILL.

In God's Gardens

O mist-blown Lily of the North,
A-bending southward in thy bloom,
And bringing beauty silver sown
And pale blue radiance of snows—

O fair white Lily, bowing low,
Above the dream-swept poppy's mouth,
Athwart the black and crimson South—
Why dost thou fear—why dost thou fear?

Lo! sense its sleep-sown subtle breath,
Where wheel in passioned whirl above
All lingering, luring love of love—
All perfume born of dole and death.

Cold ghost-wreathed Lily of the North,
When once thy dawning darkens there,
Come then with sunlight-sifted hair
And seek the haunting heaven of Night.

Where, over moon-mad shadows whirled,
The star-tanned mists dim swathe the sky
In phantasy to dream and die—
A wild sweet wedding of the World.

William Greenway

Midway

Why do I react so violently
when asked to go?
I say that it's boring,
all those rides and stalls and sausage booths,
but I don't act bored, I act mad,
still mad at the man who ran the bumper cars,
with his whiskey breath, tattooed hands
rough on my legs, getting lost, diarrhea
from the corn dogs and cotton candy,
no toilet anywhere, loud screams
from the haunted house, breaking glass,
the aisles of penned livestock,
nothing fair about it.
But most of all my parents,
not fighting now but lurching, arms
around themselves, laughing at the squirmy
canvas paintings of the freaks,
her short shorts, their faces above me
orange and blue in the midway lights,
having their ages guessed,
my mother sad because they got it right,
my father not shooting rifles or basketballs
because he knew the bears would always be
for someone else. Wooden bottles,
rubber frogs, a stage of women with the eyes
of peacock fans. But most for how
they loved it anyway, and me ashamed,
looking up, looking on. It's not the fair

so much as them I don't want to see,
tacky-loving, younger than me.

Bible Camp

I was too frail for Boy Scouts, she said,
but Bible Camp was different. Hadn't Jesus
been in the wilderness? Hadn't our ancestor
Sidney Lanier written "The Marshes of Glynn,"
where *As the marsh hen secretly builds*
on the watery sod / Behold I will build my nest
on the greatness of God? And every dawn under
the Spanish moss of my own water oak, the sky
bleeding, wouldn't I have to read my father's
Bible, with the zipper
and the tissue-thin gilt-edged leaves?

But horseflies stung me by the pool, and huge
green and purple bugs flew through the night to bang
on the screen that was half the cabin, crawled in
my bed, in the rotten egg showers.
On small islands in brackish lagoons,
wild pigs ran through our tents,
and the counselor, who heard me, homesick,
crying in the dark overhead, called me bad
sport, told how he'd swung out on the rope
above a creek and fell spread-eagled, landing
on the stump, his crotch spurting,
nearly bleeding to death.

And then it rained, and when I found it under
sandy leaves, the zipper half rusted shut,
the red words of Christ bleeding,
I cried harder.

Only Danny Clark and I didn't get Honor
Camper. *My son and Danny Clark,* my mother said.
So I never told her of the day we went
out to Jekyll Island on the yellow bus, the white
road of crushed shells a gauntlet between long
rows of palmetto and Spanish bayonet,
and we ran over the snake, a big diamondback.
I stood aside, afraid, as they
finished it off with sticks, tied it
across the fender. Somewhere
on the beach I lost my best
shirt, covered in cowboys and balloons,
looked all day, even in the pavilion
where teenagers danced and the jukebox
gave me, salty, wet, a buzz, where
the guide took the sand dollar I'd found
and said, *Here, I'll show you*
a miracle, and broke it open to get the cross
inside, then handed back the pieces.

I slept in the dunes, close as I could
to the fire, back too late from searching
to get a hot dog or blanket, crying this time
all night, shivering with cold and sand fleas.
I had stopped by the time light
came over the dunes, and I got up,
walked past the sleepers,
past the dead, smoking fire,
to where it lay, now gilded with sun,
and reached out and touched it,
ran my hand along the scales
that were dry as pages.

Winter in the South

Somewhere a thousand miles down
there's a silence between tin-roofed farms,
corn stubble, and the steel wool
of distant trees I owned on days
the gray clouds swirled and combed
like hair, lighter where the sun
yellows as it sets.

It's not cold but has been,
the clay paths spewed up
in red ice, everything still
and vertical as nails, sepia
photograph of rain. A far-off pan
of lake, cleaned of brush by the cold,
is a puddle in a yard of brown grass.

I follow trails across clearings of that
knee-high hay-grass no one knows the name of,
the arms of every oak at the woods'
edge holding shadow
like an X ray, every pine
layering its darkness. I know inside
the rusted shavings of leaves,
smell of leafmeal, broken strings
of pine needles.

Maybe one duck, circling the lake
before dark.

Walter Griffin

The Season of the Falling Face

When I am an old man
settled into myself, I will drink
whiskey from a kitchen glass
in the kitchen at night,
toast the bare bulb swinging above
my head, toast the enamel glare
of the white refrigerator light,
the cockroaches I've come to know.
I will wash my underwear in the tub,

wear headphones in the dark and listen
to the music between stations, that staticky
music found in the yellow dashlight
of travelling automobiles in the dark.
I'll sip bourbon between the mounds of covers,
swim in the flesh waters of sleep,
and in the partial light of an open doorway,
watch a man step inside his house.
I will walk my dog to the corner, her

crippled bones in love with the likes of me,
then go home to the space heater light
and listen to the rain upon the roof,
its thousands of small hands clapping down
the night and corpses of days buried
in graves as shallow as the breathing
of the dog by the fire, her eyes glazed
over, iced ponds circling stars.

Day of the Soft Mouth

"The dogs will tear 'em apart when they catch them.
But there is always a dog who will run with the rabbit,
what we call a soft mouth dog."
—(South Georgia racing dog trainer)

The hounds circle the track,
a blur of muscle and legs
stretched out in unison after
the Texas jack-rabbit; hypnotized
by the bob-tailed fur just ahead,

their bared fangs shining in
the track light of Florida dusk
while the loudspeaker blares the
numbers closing in on their prey:
Sweat glistens on the foreheads

and in the tight fisted money
hands of wild eyed men and women
screaming after their favorites.

SOMEWHERE IN THE DARK PACK
THERE IS A DOG WHO WILL NOT BITE,
WHO WILL RUN WITH THE RABBIT,
WHO MOUTHS IT LIKE BUTTER

The other dogs are not aware
of the fleet footed impostor,
hanging back and barking, the
gentle hound of a raging night
whose eyes cup the same terror

as the ragged clump of fur, now
losing the distance, reeled in
by the long legged canine and

in the kicking dust of the oval
track, the soft mouth dog waits

until the blood hour is over,
when fur and entrail disappear
on the track where he will run again,
snarling, growling and closing yet
falling back farther from the pack,
his eyes rolled back and white
like those of the rabbit, wide
and frozen like gleaming bone.

Fish Leaves

The swimming is deep in the leaves
this time of year. Back stroking
against a fall of wine colored petals
sinking silently in layers on the floor,

I circle the schools of swift moving squirrels;
gathering with me their hard shelled food.
There must be hooks waiting for them
as for me, dangling from the far side

of a flat bottomed boat, a shimmering spot
just above the surface where faceless
strangers cast their lines for wordless
mouths that open and close in the dark.

Swimming inside the noiseless shell
the sky becomes the sea and the leaves
are endless waves lapping at my chin.
There is a face bobbing in the distance,

its lip torn with hook and dying
with acorns for eyes and a nut in
its mouth while slowly sinking in the
leaves; calling my name in the cool

autumn air; waving straw like arms
all the way to the bottom. I follow
into the darkness past sound, deeper where
all words are stopped and in the skull

circling night, the water eels are my brothers
as my lifeless hulk capsizes among
the relics and seaweed. I take the hook
in the dark. The reeling takes centuries.

Georgia Douglas Johnson

Hegira

Oh, black man, why do you northward roam, and leave all the farm lands
*   bare?*
Is your house not warm, tightly thatched from storm, and a larder replete
*   your share?*
And have you not schools, fit with books and tools the steps of your young to
*   guide?*
Then what do you seek, in the north cold and bleak, 'mid the whirl of its
*   teeming tide?*

I have toiled in your cornfields, and parched in the sun, I have bowed
    'neath your load of care,
I have patiently garnered your bright golden grain, in season of storm and
    fair,
With a smile I have answered your glowering gloom, while my wounded
    heart quivering bled,
Trailing mute in your wake, as your rosy dawn breaks, while I curtain the
    mound of my dead.

Though my children are taught in the schools you have wrought, they are
    blind to the sheen of the sky,
For the brand of your hand, casts a pall o'er the land, that enshadows the
    gleam of the eye,
My sons, deftly sapped of the brawn-hood of man, self-rejected and
    impotent stand,
My daughters, unhaloed, unhonored, undone, feed the lust of a dominant
    land.

I would not remember, yet could not forget, how the hearts beating true
    to your own,

You've tortured, and wounded, and filtered their blood 'til a budding
    Hegira has blown.

Unstrange is the pathway to Calvary's hill, which I wend in my dumb
    agony,
Up its perilous height, in the pale morning light, to dissever my own from
    the tree.

And so I'm away, where the sky-line of day sets the arch of its rainbow
    afar,
To the land of the north, where the symbol of worth sets the broad gates
    of combat ajar!

The Octoroon

One drop of midnight in the dawn of life's pulsating stream
Marks her an alien from her kind, a shade amid its gleam;
Forevermore her step she bends insular, strange, apart—
And none can read the riddle of her wildly warring heart.

The stormy current of her blood beats like a mighty sea
Against the man-wrought iron bars of her captivity.
For refuge, succor, peace and rest, she seeks that humble fold
Whose every breath is kindliness, whose hearts are purest gold.

Black Woman

Don't knock at my door, little child,
    I cannot let you in,
You know not what a world this is
    Of cruelty and sin.
Wait in the still eternity
    Until I come to you,

The world is cruel, cruel, child,
    I cannot let you in!

Don't knock at my heart, little one,
    I cannot bear the pain
Of turning deaf-ear to your call
    Time and time again!
You do not know the monster men
    Inhabiting the earth,
Be still, be still, my precious child,
    I must not give you birth!

When I Rise Up

When I rise above the earth,
And look down on the things that fetter me,
I beat my wings upon the air,
Or tranquil lie,
Surge after surge of potent strength
Like incense comes to me
When I rise up above the earth
And look down upon the things that fetter me.

Greg Johnson

The Foreign Element

So briefly we detained him in the hall,
asked Why? Why?—not using even that word
but only the kind of shell-shocked glare
these medical veterans dread, especially near
dinner time. Sighing, he faced a quick-witted blond aunt
and two blond cousins, a gaunt lover with rings
under his eyes, and three others lacking acknowledged
relevance or rank (we took turns delivering coffee)—
yet at least the mother lay resting, in a spare bed
downstairs. "Think of it," he said, again,
"as a foreign element in the blood, against which we have
no defenses." Giddy with sorrow, I thought
We have no defenses, yes we have no bananas,
as he added, impossibly, "We're doing all we can."

The aunt, whom I'd gotten to know and dislike,
marched back to Intensive Care when the white-coat
left, heels clattering like a small child's drums
as if *she'd* defend him, by God, but then stopped short
and threw herself in a nearby chair. The cousins
attended this new display of grief, while the lover
wandered off without meeting anyone's eyes
and we three milled without aim, as usual, becoming
foreign ourselves in this timeless fluorescent world
where the random invaded bodies come to die. Later,
we'd draw straws to see who would bear
the nightly non-news to his mother downstairs, recalling
all the way down
that in old times, when they killed

their messengers, words had a harsh, consoling power,
surging in the blood and cruelly expressed
in that thrilling reprimand.
Now, speaking a foreign language, we stare
at one another, useless, as we await another death
with its casual pomp and non-dramatic flair,
its message we don't dare to understand.

A Death That Dare Not Speak . . .

Smooth-cheeked, bright-eyed, dying,
you joked that here was the death
that dare not speak its name—
for you were twenty-three, and a poet,
so you reveled in the unspeakable
and took the irony as your proper due.
Your languishing idols, gape-mouthed Chatterton
or gasping Keats, translated their last breaths into
posterity, but no fame would attend
your deathbed, only your plentiful kin.
Your mother from Dallas. Siblings from Fort Worth,
Austin, New Haven. All were flying in.

"He doesn't *look* sick," your mother confided in me
the day they wheeled you into Intensive Care,
"do you think that perhaps . . . ?" That perhaps
it was all some poetic fancy the child in you
concocted out of the headlines and your infamous
need for attention? "You know," she added,
"he hasn't basically changed since he was four."

You could never speak lies, and the doctor
did not, but I overheard your married orthodontist brother
hiss at her ear that penultimate night, "What will we
tell them back home?" You were worlds away from her answer.

Jobless and beautiful, now you lay comatose
in your dreams of pathos and fame, believing
your name would eclipse *its* name, eventually,
never mind that you hadn't yet gotten around
to writing anything. "Genius knows itself, right?"
you'd said slyly, not offering any more,
for you were strategic in your refusals, living
a sibylline text we mortals could never interpret.
But neither could we parse the doctor's language
when he whispered of "internal lesions," groping through
such ugly syllables as were, themselves, "gnawing
insults to the brain"—a sort of found poetry
of the kind so common in your last days,
like the white phrases of the nurses' shoes
as they passed down the hall, or your mother's sobbing refrain
as she held your hand, so cool and forever stilled.

So that last day's ordeal ground on, your family and friends
hopeful one moment, the next dulled by sorrow. Hourly
the doctor was beggared for scraps of good news; hourly
your past or would-be lovers, eyes ringed
from wordless brooding at the brink of loss,
arrived with their small talk. Your mother
did crosswords, laughed, or wept. Your favorite
orthodontist sat grinding his teeth, while your
pretty college-age sisters drowsed
over geometry texts and *The Mill on the Floss.*
Near the end, your mother cried out, "But he never
said anything, it just isn't fair!"—though by now
even this seemed part of the general drone,
and vaguely I thought that your coma had seeped
inside the waiting room like a merciful gas,
attenuating all our words and gestures
into these last faint cries of protest.

As you would have wanted, no one spoke
when the end did come, though we circled your bed

as though expecting nothing short of revelation
to issue from those lips so often pursed
in mockery, mirth, or small sighs of pleasure.
A tease to the last, you seemed only kiddingly dead
as you drained all the love in the room
the way Narcissus absorbed whole pools
into himself. But the surface stayed unbroken,
the charm intact. When I tried to summon words
of solace or devotion, my mind went numb, could only
repeat in dazed and rude abandon, *The end, the end.*
Your mother and sisters wept, but still no one
dared utter a word
as you drifted off into legend.

Sidney Lanier

The Marshes of Glynn

Glooms of the live-oaks, beautiful-braided and woven
With intricate shades of the vines that myriad-cloven
   Clamber the forks of the multiform boughs,—
           Emerald twilights,—
           Virginal shy lights,
Wrought of the leaves to allure to the whisper of vows,
When lovers pace timidly down through the green colonnades
Of the dim sweet woods, of the dear dark woods,
   Of the heavenly woods and glades,
That run to the radiant marginal sand-beach within
     The wide sea-marshes of Glynn;—

Beautiful glooms, soft dusks in the noon-day fire,—
Wildwood privacies, closets of lone desire,
Chamber from chamber parted with wavering arras of leaves,—
Cells for the passionate pleasure of prayer to the soul that grieves,
Pure with a sense of the passing of saints through the wood,
Cool for the dutiful weighing of ill with good;—

O braided dusks of the oak and woven shades of the vine,
While the riotous noon-day sun of the June-day long did shine
Ye held me fast in your heart and I held you fast in mine;
But now when the noon is no more, and riot is rest,
And the sun is a-wait at the ponderous gate of the West,
And the slant yellow beam down the wood-aisle doth seem
Like a lane into heaven that leads from a dream,—
Ay, now, when my soul all day hath drunken the soul of the oak,
And my heart is at ease from men, and the wearisome sound of the stroke

Of the scythe of time and the trowel of trade is low,
  And belief overmasters doubt, and I know that I know,
  And my spirit is grown to a lordly great compass within,
That the length and the breadth and the sweep of the marshes of Glynn
Will work me no fear like the fear they have wrought me of yore
When length was fatigue, and when breadth was but bitterness sore,
And when terror and shrinking and dreary unnamable pain
Drew over me out of the merciless miles of the plain,—

Oh, now, unafraid, I am fain to face
  The vast sweet visage of space.
To the edge of the wood I am drawn, I am drawn,
Where the gray beach glimmering runs, as a belt of the dawn,
  For a mete and a mark
    To the forest-dark:—
        So:
Affable live-oak, leaning low,—
Thus—with your favor—soft, with a reverent hand,
(Not lightly touching your person, Lord of the land!)
Bending your beauty aside, with a step I stand
On the firm-packed sand,
            Free
By a world of marsh that borders a world of sea.
  Sinuous southward and sinuous northward the shimmering band
    Of the sand-beach fastens the fringe of the marsh to the folds of the
      land.
Inward and outward to northward and southward the beach-lines linger
      and curl
As a silver-wrought garment that clings to and follows the firm sweet
      limbs of a girl.
Vanishing, swerving, evermore curving again into sight,
Softly the sand-beach wavers away to a dim gray looping of light.
And what if behind me to westward the wall of the woods stands high?
The world lies east: how ample, the marsh and the sea and the sky!
A league and a league of marsh-grass, waist-high, broad in the blade,
Green, and all of a height, and unflecked with a light or a shade,

Stretch leisurely off, in a pleasant plain,
To the terminal blue of the main.

Oh, what is abroad in the marsh and the terminal sea?
   Somehow my soul seems suddenly free
From the weighing of fate and the sad discussion of sin,
By the length and the breadth and the sweep of the marshes of Glynn.

Ye marshes, how candid and simple and nothing-withholding and free
Ye publish yourselves to the sky and offer yourselves to the sea!
Tolerant plains, that suffer the sea and the rains and the sun,
Ye spread and span like the catholic man who hath mightily won
God out of knowledge and good out of infinite pain
And sight out of blindness and purity out of a stain.

As the marsh-hen secretly builds on the watery sod,
Behold I will build me a nest on the greatness of God:
I will fly in the greatness of God as the marsh-hen flies
In the freedom that fills all the space 'twixt the marsh and the skies:
By so many roots as the marsh-grass sends in the sod
I will heartily lay me a-hold on the greatness of God:
Oh, like to the greatness of God is the greatness within
The range of the marshes, the liberal marshes of Glynn.

And the sea lends large, as the marsh: lo, out of his plenty the sea
Pours fast: full soon the time of the flood-tide must be:
Look how the grace of the sea doth go
About and about through the intricate channels that flow
    Here and there,
          Everywhere,
Till his waters have flooded the uttermost creeks and the low-lying lanes,
And the marsh is meshed with a million veins,
That like as with rosy and silvery essences flow
    In the rose-and-silver evening glow.
          Farewell, my lord Sun!
The creeks overflow: a thousand rivulets run

'Twixt the roots of the sod; the blades of the marsh-grass stir;
Passeth a hurrying sound of wings that westward whirr:
Passeth, and all is still; and the currents cease to run;
And the sea and the marsh are one.

How still the plains of the waters be!
The tide is in his ecstasy.
The tide is at his highest height:
   And it is night.

And now from the Vast of the Lord will the waters of sleep
Roll in on the souls of men,
But who will reveal to our waking ken
The forms that swim and the shapes that creep
   Under the waters of sleep?
And I would I could know what swimmeth below when the tide comes in
On the length and the breadth of the marvellous marshes of Glynn.

Song of the Chattahoochee

 Out of the hills of Habersham,
  Down the valleys of Hall,
I hurry amain to reach the plain,
Run the rapid and leap the fall,
Split at the rock and together again,
Accept my bed, or narrow or wide,
And flee from folly on every side
With a lover's pain to attain the plain
  Far from the hills of Habersham,
  Far from the valleys of Hall.

 All down the hills of Habersham,
  All through the valleys of Hall,
The rushes cried *Abide, abide,*
The willful waterweeds held me thrall,
The laving laurel turned my tide,

The ferns and the fondling grass said *Stay,*
The dewberry dipped for to work delay,
And the little reeds sighed *Abide, abide,*
  Here in the hills of Habersham,
  Here in the valleys of Hall.

  High o'er the hills of Habersham,
  Veiling the valleys of Hall,
The hickory told me manifold
Fair tales of shade, the poplar tall
Wrought me her shadowy self to hold,
The chestnut, the oak, the walnut, the pine,
Overleaning, with flickering meaning and sign,
Said, *Pass not, so cold, these manifold*
  Deep shades of the hills of Habersham,
  These glades in the valleys of Hall.

  And oft in the hills of Habersham,
  And oft in the valleys of Hall,
The white quartz shone, and the smooth brook-stone
Did bar me of passage with friendly brawl,
And many a luminous jewel lone
—Crystals clear or a-cloud with mist,
Ruby, garnet and amethyst—
Made lures with the lights of streaming stone
  In the clefts of the hills of Habersham,
  In the beds of the valleys of Hall.

  But oh, not the hills of Habersham,
  And oh, not the valleys of Hall
Avail: I am fain for to water the plain.
Downward the voices of Duty call—
Downward, to toil and be mixed with the main,
The dry fields burn, and the mills are to turn,
And a myriad flowers mortally yearn,
And the lordly main from beyond the plain
  Calls o'er the hills of Habersham,
  Calls through the valleys of Hall.

Thar's More in the Man Than Thar Is in the Land

I knowed a man, which he lived in Jones,
Which Jones is a county of red hills and stones,
And he lived pretty much by gittin' of loans,
And his mules was nuthin' but skin and bones,
And his hogs was flat as his corn-bread pones,
And he had 'bout a thousand acres o' land.

This man—which his name it was also Jones—
He swore that he'd leave them old red hills and stones,
Fur he couldn't make nuthin' but yallerish cotton,
And little *o' that,* and his fences was rotten,
And what little corn he had, *hit* was boughten
And dinged ef a livin' was in the land.

And the longer he swore the madder he got,
And he riz and he walked to the stable lot,
And he hollered to Tom to come thar and hitch
Fur to emigrate somewhar whar land was rich,
And to quit raisin' cock-burrs, thistles and sich,
And a wastin' ther time on the cussed land.

So him and Tom they hitched up the mules,
Pertestin' that folks was mighty big fools
That 'ud stay in Georgy their lifetime out,
Jest scratchin' a livin' when all of 'em mought
Git places in Texas whar cotton would sprout
By the time you could plant it in the land.

And he driv by a house whar a man named Brown
Was a livin', not fur from the edge o' town,
And he bantered Brown fur to buy his place,
And said that bein' as money was skace,
And bein' as sheriffs was hard to face,
Two dollars an acre would git the land.

They closed at a dollar and fifty cents,
And Jones he bought him a waggin and tents,
And loaded his corn, and his wimmin, and truck,
And moved to Texas, which it tuck
His entire pile, with the best of luck,
To git thar and git him a little land.

But Brown moved out on the old Jones' farm,
And he rolled up his breeches and bared his arm,
And he picked all the rocks from off'n the groun',
And he rooted it up and he plowed it down,
Then he sowed his corn and his wheat in the land.

Five years glid by, and Brown, one day
(Which he'd got so fat that he wouldn't weigh),
Was a settin' down, sorter lazily,
To the bulliest dinner you ever see,
When one o' the children jumped on his knee
And says, "Yan's Jones, which you bought his land."

And thar was Jones, standin' out at the fence,
And he hadn't no waggin, nor mules, nor tents,
Fur he had left Texas afoot and cum
To Georgy to see if he couldn't git sum
Employment, and he was a lookin' as hum-
Ble as ef he had never owned any land.

But Brown he axed him in, and he sot
Him down to his vittles smokin' hot,
And when he had filled hisself and the floor
Brown looked at him sharp and riz and swore
That, "whether men's land was rich or poor
Thar was more in the *man* than thar was in the *land*."

Frank Manley

Origin of the Species

Dogs are all doomed.
They cannot survive.
They screw your guests
Below the knees
And hump the furniture.
They shit in the streets
And piss on small children.
Sometimes they eat them.
They also eat garbage.
Dogs have bad breath.
Their eyes are sad.
They sleep in the sun
And need to be consoled.

Dogs are like dinosaurs.
The last ones are shrinking.
They never go out.
They sit in your lap
And smell good.
They have no fleas,
Nothing to bark at.
They turn into cats.

And the cats will survive.
They shit in boxes
And cover it up.
They are always alone.
Cats are like grease.

They make no noise.
They care about nothing.
Cats stay in houses
And never get lost.
They look out of windows.
They are always thinking.
Cats are like people.
Cats will inherit the earth.

Blackberries

When they're in at the cove as long as my thumb,
I say to my knuckle-faced fist full of neighbors,
Like a hound that's been beaten a little too hard,
"A smart man hadn't got sense how to grow them."

They smile like splits in a piece of pine.

But they come. They put down the fields
That harrow them clean of briars and weeds,
They cut loose the tractors to run with the dogs,
And they come and stand around for a while
With nothing to do and no way to do it.
They grow into ease like an empty field,
In patches of talk, with buckets and hip boots
And long hungry bellies for what you can't
Grow and can't hardly chew up and swallow—
For pinecones and briars and knotweeds and rocks,
Whatever tastes wild and goes down hard.

We drink at the spring and talk about snakes.

Above the spring the cove lies low,
Still as a snake in its coil of land.

We wade in the canes till they're over our heads,
And one by one they swallow us whole
Till no one is left but each one alone,
Chained to the spot of our mortal flesh
By the sinewy whiplash we stir up around us
And eating as fast as our hands can move,

Full of the taste of hard-bitten things.

We sweat in the stillness and bleed in the quiet,
Filling like summer and almost as slow,
Till one by one we explode into walking
And startle ourselves to come back again.
We gather together like parts of a body
Fresh risen, uncertain of where they fit in,
And drink us some whiskey to settle our brains.
We talk about hunting and fishing and women
And what we have gotten and what we can't get.

The whippoorwills finally use up the daylight.

At home in the lamplight the berries flash dark
In the well of the buckets like droppings of day.
In the sweat of the kitchens the women prepare them
And render them harmless as good as they can
With sacksful of sugar and thick crusts of pastry
That pop your teeth open, sprouting with seeds,
While out in the parlors the men drink more whiskey
And stare at the windows that stare back at them.
They wash off the rank smell they carry
Inside them and sleep with their women,
A tangle of still canes that gleam in the moonlight,

Dreaming of nothing, gone wild again.

First Eclogue

When I was a boy, lean and tough as thought,
The dogs were still at Emory, and I would
Read in the marble library all day
Till the grass and the trees and the sky were changed
And burst with light in the slanting sun, each
Pine top spiked with gold, each leaf transparent.
Or I would sing in my carrel all summer
While the dogs slept on in the shadowed grass.
Pleased with the shade in the marble cool world
I slept like the dogs who slept like God—my wife
Young and beautiful and the dogs sleeping under
The trees, in the halls, or on the worn marble stairs.
They slept through all my years at school,
A changing pack of hounds and feists, setters
And beagles, groaning and stretching and farting in quiet,
Each in his solitude, while overhead
Ancient voices moved through waves of heat:
Nos patriae fines, et dulcia linquimus arva;
Nos patriam fugimus.

Wilderness

On 5 May 1864
When Abner Small went out to look for men who had run
The darkness he moved in was visible

Humps of honeysuckle
Hung from the trees like sharpshooters
The underbrush huddled like lines of skirmishers
And everywhere the fires
The wounded crept about like flames
And the animals were gone

And only the night remained there
Only the smoke like the smell of darkness
Whole pine trees burned like candles

When Abner Small went out into the Wilderness
Looking for men on their feet still running
He saw a shell burst overhead
Like a great comet or bolt of lightning
The darkness lifted
And he saw before him the trees appear
Each vine each leaf each blade of grass
Distinct in the overwhelming light
He startled at the sudden glare
And kicked up the smoldering flames in the leafmold
A shower of sparks flew out from his feet
Like footsteps his spirit took
Like the footprints of his soul before him

And he saw a man with red hair and beard
He lay like a pile of dead leaves
A mound of briars or honeysuckle
The flames reached him
They lit in his beard and his beard burned
His red hair flamed
And the cartridges at his belt exploded
And Abner Small saw in the new light
Who the man looked like
His beard and red hair
He saw his own side explode
And his own eyes stare at himself
And discovered the man he was sent for

And in the quick light of the shell
He saw a white dogwood in bloom
The pale flowers red in the firelight
He saw the whole tree blossom at once
Leaf bole fuse and flower

In one blinding moment of light
Like the petals of the soul
Burning inside him
As the flames licked the tips of his eyes
And the glowing coals touched his lips
He heard a voice from the burning bush
Like the sound of his breath
Inward and outward
Saying forever
I am who am
I am who am

Frances Mayes

Shaving My Legs with Ockham's Razor

From the dream world of paradigms
    I took the water slide: a decade of realism

Brings me to William, his steady truth
    that the world proceeds case by case.

Take my legs—winter pale, glowing like white
    neon. The long bone an arctic ledge

Propped and glistening on the tub—
    William could have regarded them, instead of Plato's beard

That never could come off. Every three days, I lather
    the faint stubble, dip my disposable razor:

If less is enough, why do more?
    He must have honed his razor on a thick strop.

I'm steeped these late sensible years
    in his principle of parsimony, so close to parsnip and parson.

There once was a paradigm! My legs tanned and oiled.
    Shaved daily—such perfection:

Buttered in summer with cocoanut oil,
    (toenails scarlet), slicked in winter with lotions.

Moreover, what to say about that ultra-idealist, Aunt Emmy,
    who plucked out each hair on her legs with tweezers:

Never shave; it will grow back thick and black.
  I watched to see if her pores enlarged but no,

When the creamy pegnoir fell to the side I saw her calves
  silky firm and slim. *Suffer for beauty,* she said.

But William, after my father's, I borrowed your razor!
  A straight edge. Your cool, fetid breath in my face:

Plurality is not to be assumed without necessity.
  My legs in perfection at Bowen's Mill swimming pool.

My legs at the end of exhausting winter, daikon roots.
  William, old heretic, you died

The Black Death, that quick wasting. I would like to get out
  Of this tub. Scraped clean, I will slip into a skirt

With a flounce and walk down the white road into town.
  Oil of narcissus on my pulse points, radiating *more is more.*

Etruscan Head

You, plowing,
turn up a marble head
in the furrow. It is 1790
and raining. She broke true
at the neck, looks back
at the sky with eyes
emptied of time older than
the Romans. Nose sheared
but the bridge high and fine,
the mouth like the mouth
of the nervy village girl
who steals your grapes and cuts

her eyes at you.
Sweat runs down your back.
The head has come up
clean. It feels fresh and
heavy in your hands. What to do
with the broken beauty of the past?
You place the head
on an olive stump and under
the rain she begins to shine,
heroic, moon pure, your dead
daughter's forehead, a peel
of wax on the cathedral floor.
Your clothes stink and steam.
Now you take the plow and
follow the hillside. Two hundred
years later I will see her
in the Volterra museum.
My grandmother's blind eyes
come back to stare. I would
like to hold the head, I
think her shoulders
would feel like mine.
Somewhere under the vineyards
I imagine perfect hard
hands and sandaled feet.
We're not mistaken about our lives.

Good Friday, Driving Home

Not travelling; getting there. Traffic
Pouring into blinding light. But the fog
Looks enlightened, roiling over the hills.
Angels might appear in a chariot
With news of the open-ended universe.

The groove I've worn down this road.
Back lit sky, are houses near the coast
Blazing? My mind drags the pavement
Like a string of tin cans. There, those beautiful
Horses, six, seven, grazing along the reservoir.
One is a palomino. Of course, of course
They remind me. The sight, ice on the heart.
Memory, that guerrilla keeps lighting smoky fires.
Those lost could do worse than be recalled
By horses in spring grass, could do worse
Than own all shaded streets, lilacs, crescent
Moon, and sailboats. Who do I think they are,
Saints, with their emblems? I'm affected by
Silvered sky, this drastic day mad with
Traffic. Years gone I memorized Donne:
Restore thine Image, so much, by thy grace,
That thou may'st know mee, and I'll turne my face.
Westward, westward, things in motion stay in motion.
I roll down the window, watch for cars swerving
To the wrong lane. So many of us alone. Compact.
Good mileage. We fail and can tell ourselves nothing.
We break apart and invent
Why. We place our faith. Lose track. Blinker flashing,
Keep left. I am totally emptied and must
Fill myself again. The racing of powerful,
Unlovely emotions. What is the endless world?
Comes around again the cusp of summer.
I still like linen. Peach colored linen. I think
Of tanning my legs. I feel the word *prayer*
In my mind. Just the word. A smooth river stone.
I'm accomplishing the miles to San Francisco
For the thousandth time, add them to my *vita.*
I'm better off than Mona's mother with her hair
In curl papers thirty years, waiting for the occasion.
I have occasion. Press on. Oh soul of mud.
Half of what sacrifice ransoms us?

Snapshots: Annie Davis

She is over-exposed
in that reductive winter light
She seems all shoulder pads and lipstick
against a bank of snow

She was my aunt
who went north and
sent back one photograph
"She's pale as a mushroom"
my mother said
Grandmother tried to see beneath her hat
"I believe she has dyed her hair
What is that girl dreaming of"
My mother said she was brazen
she'd married beneath her
and would live to regret it

Later she used to call at midnight
her hoarse voice full of gin
and the New York winter nights
in towns we'd never heard of
We were children
who never had seen snow
"What's it like up there" I'd say
"When are you coming home"

Sometimes she dropped the phone
it beat like a metronome
against the wall of some bar
We'd hear laughter far away and music
then someone would curse
and slam down the phone

Afterwards I asked what those words meant
"It was a crackle in the line"
my mother said
"we were cut off
and don't pick up the extension again"
When she died there
no one would say why
It was as though this time
she'd gone too far
I asked if she'd lived
to regret it

I thought she was buried
in the snowbank that spring would melt
Then she would come home
wearing her red dress
when she stepped off the train
full of news

Susie Mee

From My Grandmother's Diary, West Armuchee, Georgia, 1887

"The last time I saw you
it was raining
and the road through the valley
had melted to clay.
When I stepped from the carriage—breathless
from holding your hand—
the leaves on the fig trees
seemed bright as hummingbirds.
When you left
without saying goodbye
Uncle Boris said it was sheer
negligence and best forgotten.
All day I threw stones into the creek
with a vengeance, walking
backwards on them without falling.
In the fields, I blew hundreds of cotton bolls into the air,
each time calling your name."

Mules in New York

I see them in some procession of the dead
halfway between day and night, scattering butterflies,
their hooves hammering diamonds into the cement.

Why do I bring them here?
Why send them meandering down Fifth Avenue,
or trotting up to Central Park
for a draft of lake water?

Instead, why not let them be content
in that other dream: munching grass
beside a dirt road in Georgia?

Howard Beach, Bensonhurst, Etc.

In these times of latent violence, hearkening back
to distant injustices, the past, like a reel of film,
has a way of winding down to a negative vision,
proving once again (if proof be needed)
that every sentiment—both the one displaced
and the one displacing—contains
its own irony;
and no generation can be sure
that the dream it needs
may not be the one
by which someone else
is dying.

Judson Mitcham

Notes for a Prayer in June

1

                  The other boys lived,
and a prayer grew from this:
the unbelievable sadness of chance
and the shattering dazzle of glass still strewn,
days later, on the road.

2

My son won't let things go, and I love
his fighting to understand, in his own terms.
Having learned about light years, he recalled
the distance to the school, how heavy
his legs felt when he raced there.

                      What form
will his knowledge of the wreck take,
when he learns how, late one Sunday,
twenty Junes ago now, I flung you from the world,
through a windshield?

                Will I tell him
how I ran to get help,
yet tired, had to slow down, my legs turned to lead,
had to rest in the face of death, how far
I have traveled through the years?

3

I remember the late spring night we camped out
on Alcovy Mountain, just the three of us
who later on would take that ride.
We laughed at ourselves for playing war.

We were nearly sixteen.
And it seems like a last act of childhood,
crawling up the north slope
so softly I could reach for a branch,
draw a bead down its gnarled barrel
and laugh you dead.
      The next morning
when absolute darkness had failed, for a while,
we stood without words above the world,
a white mist drifting far beneath us
forever, over homes we were headed for.

4

Is it breath rising in the Christmas air
as a child pedals up and down the driveway at dawn?
Is it dizziness with which
a woman has to reach for the words
to send into silence with her son?
       Each June,
it's the brief taste of salt, licked away,
as a boy hurries out to the street, having breezed
through the hot kitchen, kissed his mother's face.

5

Before our eyes, that heavy old coin disappears,
while it stays where it is. We're aware
sundown is a lie now,
though we see it the same. Chimpanzees
pause, sometimes, from their foraging or play,
sit quietly and gaze into the west
until moved by darkness.
      Perhaps, in their eyes,
nothing seems magical, or it all does. From us
comes a forced, final nod toward the sleight
of relentless method, how it turns
pure mystery to laughter in the end.

Still,
we know there's a magic we begin with, tricked
by love's act into this ruled world.

　　　　　—for Glenn Hawkins, Jr.

Night Ride, 1965

Exactly at one o'clock,
I crawl out, walk the half mile to the dirt road,
wait for the loud DeSoto, its gold now sanded dull brown,
color of damp pine straw. When the car slows,
dust catches up, steams forward through the headlights,
into the dark. The farm station signed off for hours,
all the others too remote for the aerial,
the radio's faint rasped harmony's lost
to the car's bass throb. As we cross the main road,
we can look down at the small town's single row of stores,
streetlights blazing like a runway
only the desperate or crazed would try to land on,
and we cruise all night down narrow county roads,
talking as though we could say it all, could tell
what it means to grow quiet at the first light,
while the stars all fail, what it means
finally to turn home
with the clear crackle of tires rising from the wet road,
as sweet cut fields come cool through rolled-down windows.

Somewhere in Ecclesiastes

Accident
A kitten, startled onto the stove, tips over
a pan of boiling water.
And a little boy, weakened by his burns, must surrender

to pneumonia, must become
a piece of deep blue in the puzzle
his mother hasn't yet put together. He is sky,

surely, but the kitten—what is it?
A diagonal of rain? Does she have to fit it in—
the streak of soft gray? Who will tell her?

Her friends have faith in mysterious ways.
They say it, and they say it, until God
himself kicks the handle of the pan. And for her,

all the colors turn ugly and cruel unless
there is chaos at the root of every beauty—she is wild,
remembering his eyes—and we are blessed

only by accident, only by chance.

Soul
What if it were true, after all,
that the body is a garment, a light cotton shirt
we will easily do without?

If we knew this beyond any question,
would it alter the funerals of children?

                                        Imagine
a world in which the mother of a seven-year-old
who was killed in a wreck doesn't come
from the new grave feeling like a woman

who struggles up out of a lake, soaked,
wearing everything she owns,
and who can't take anything off, not a scarf,
not a ludicrous hat with a feather.

What
if the body were a silk slip lifted in the hands
of a lover, then tossed on the floor,
with a laugh?

Sunday

1

With six young blacks at the door of the church,
suddenly, in 1963,
and the preacher out of town, the decision
fell to you, as the chairman of the deacons.

You took them down the aisle, and I recall
you put them on the left, second pew,
in the same place Ben and I had waited,
at ages three and four, for the anthem
to be over. You would come down from the choir
to sit between us then.
                              I couldn't quit
glancing at the visitors,
who gave away nothing, not a trace
of the strain they must have felt.
                              That Sunday,
across the kitchen table, we agreed,
intensely, on the clarity of scripture:
"My house shall be a house of prayer . . .
all ye who labor and are heavy laden . . .
knock, and it shall be opened."

The congregation voted two to one
only one week later to exclude
Negroes from the services,
                              and soon—
confused by many things I couldn't name—

I would find this hypocrisy convenient
as the reason I would leave the Baptist church
or any other faith. I made you pay
for staying on. What did I desire?

A man in a signboard trumpeting "Repent"
on the corner of the all-white church? Perhaps.
But I made this judgment from the sofa,
while watching old movies on the TV,
                                        reading
the fat Sunday paper,
starting with the comics and the sports.
2
A Sunday is a parable of time, always was.

In the hard-shell old days,
you couldn't drag a stick across the dirt.
The stick became a plow, the mark a furrow.

We heard those stories from your mother,
having traveled to her house after church, to sit,
forever, in the parlor, underneath
the portrait of a stern young man
at the center of the mantel.
                              Legend had it
dancing got him turned out of the church.
Your father, in his coffin twenty years
when I was born, loved the mandolin
and the banjo that could bring him to his feet.

I like to think of that. And of the Sundays
when men played semipro ball on the mill field,
doubleheaders stretching into dusk,
into chimes coming soft over the pines, *sweet hour
of prayer.*
            Best of all, I remember
a pitcher with a slowness close to magical—

knuckleball, palm ball, sinker,
butterflies he fluttered at the batter.
                              Back then,
following the evening benediction,
often we would drive through the center of Monroe—
ghostly in its calm—
to the only place open, the Trailways station,
for the ice cream cones we had to eat

strategically and fast, that sweetness which began
melting as we took it in our hands.

3
This is partly explained, I am told, by the tricky
physiology of shock:
                    I reacted
as though I had heard good news—a bizarre
confusion on a day of great clarity, with each
blossom of wild red clover, every breath
and bony arm sharply redefined. I had heard
my brother say thickly,
"He's gone."
              There are those
who insist the word *love* explains nothing,
but is only a maneuver, like music, in the effort
to follow what the body figures out. Who has not
believed each move of a dream

till instructed by his name, or the daybreak? Who,
having reached my age, hasn't once
grown silent while the talk trickled on, got a look
at the faces of bone, then turned
with an ache to say it all?
                          Here's a story
I'd forgotten: early August in the Philippines, you
with CQ duty, while your buddies trucked off
to the show. Kay Kyser, at the close,

had stood with his arms wide, sobbing, to announce
it was over.
                    So the men came back
dancing in the street, some choking out prayers
or running just to run, others quieter than ever,
observing themselves, oddly frightened.
                                    When Ben
telephoned the news,
euphoria appalled me, joy washed over
my body. I'm unable to explain. I'd believe,
if I could, in the shock of sudden victory.
                                    The only
word I have is *love*.

4
A sophomore stuffed with philosophy,
                                    home
from college on the weekends,
I cultivated arguments with you, attempts to show
the doubtful ontology of heaven.
Not arguments exactly—I would lecture, and you
would sit there listening, at times
asking me a question.
                    When the honeymoon
of grief left off, when I quit
letting go on the back road, headed for work,
or waking in the night, on my feet,
as if the telephone had rung,
                            I discovered
anger like a child's pure fury
at a simple recognition—the authority, say,
of gravity or sleep.
                    I am kneeling
at the grave, with a butcher knife in hand,
hacking at the dark fist of ice
that won't turn loose of the yellow silk flowers
we buried in the vase last summer.

Finally, it splits. Lynda kneels
with the bright poinsettia for the cylinder.

When you came to get us up, Sunday mornings,
for a few years there—it became a family joke—
you did it on cue:

the Lefevres sang "*I'll* fly away . . ." signing off
a half hour of gospel on the radio. Why
do I think about this, still gripping the knife,

having nothing else to hit, with such a purpose?

5
Instead of heading home, one Sunday at noon,
we turned up 138, and we stopped
at a family place, east of Conyers.

But Mama didn't really have an appetite. To me,
it was army food—greasy, mass-produced.
The restaurant was hot, the lighting harsh,
the tables too close, and the single price high.

I took her to the other side of town,
to the small monastery she had never seen,
and neither had I, in the early afternoon,
when the sun angled down through the windows,
indigo and gold on the chapel floor.

A man walked alone through the sanctuary,
never looking up.
                    On the road
to Monroe, fields of goldenrod flickered
in the wind. When I wondered out loud
about the name of that weed,
she told me what it was, without surprise.

And I think about a morning at the old house,
of you and me looking at a spider web
delicate with light.
I reached out to tear the thing down,
and you caught me by the wrist.
                              If I believe
it was not a bright pain
that made your eyes open on a Sunday
in April, who will stop me? If I name

the day itself, the day of rest, the dust,

the silver-white filaments of dust floating down,
slowly, like a dream of falling snow,
through the avenue of light by the bed.
                              If I say
it was this that took your breath.

Marion Montgomery

Aunt Emma, Uncle Al: A Short History of the South

My Uncle Al on Saturday night lay warmly in the ditch and Sunday
  morning saw the Lordly Tisking churchward
While Aunt Emma kept the sentimental lamp bright into breakfast;

And Sunday morning Uncle Al tied grannyknots and squareknots and
  flipped nickels up his sleeve. He told about that marvelous old unicorn,
  the hoop snake of the ivory horn and apple tree
While Aunt Emma piled plates, rejoicing Uncle Al out under arbor
  shooting marbles with his boys;

And Uncle Al called quail up in the orchard in the afternoon and sang the
  moon up with his brood around him on the steps
While Aunt Emma bathed the barefoot sleepy feet;

Until a solemn Sunday when the Lordly Tisking raised my Uncle Al up
  from the ditch. The two to twelve to teens scrubbed necks for Sunday
  School while Aunt sweating Emma fried chicken for my Lordly Tisking
  Uncle Al.

Lost marbles, squareknots only, and the aphids sucked the scuppernongs.

And when Aunt Emma died with cancer of the womb the three to teens
  began to scatter like flushed quail

And all my Uncle Al's sharp evening calling never brought them back to
  roost again.

Lines for Ben Slaughter

Hunter, Woodsman, Farmer; Killed by a
Falling Tree, November 9, 1954

The lone hounds holler under the moon,
The leaves flow wild with a wild wild sound,
And the black owl hovers motionless
Where one tall pine tree measures ground.

The lean coon pants in a hollow log
And rests all night from the swamp-slow run;
The sharp hawk whets his beak on bark
High in the frost-sharp light of the sun.

And the nights and days flow end to end,
The owl, the coon, the hawk wax fat,
And the tall tree moulders on the floor
In Ben Slaughter's native habitat.

Fishing Cloud Creek, Oglethorpe County August under Thunderheads

The summer of plowed fields settles quietly behind us.
　　It is my fortieth year. The air is like sediment.

I have seen the bones of a leaf in a stone.

Upstream, the disturbing thought of the water: a birch leaf, boned like the
　　dorsal of bream, roils up; curves lost in a swirl.
Over slow stones, bruising as leaves bruise, through lean roots as the tree
　　leans. It finally settles in sand here before me. Whorled foam thickens
　　where my cork waits.

"But why does it smell like wild honey?"

Hush, child. How can I tell such long stories as bees among alien birches?
My bones know impossible answers. Words waste—the journey of
water.

"Don't dabble your pole in the water. Soon bream will be biting."

Promise, and the tall clouds, frowning.

Eric Nelson

Three Die in Seconds

I'm sorry for the dead,
but they're something else now.
No one can assume their posture,
the way their feet seem
jammed inside the wrong shoes,
arms screwed into stripped threads.

The illusion I can't follow
is a picture of three men
soon dead by explosion
standing quietly outside
an embassy in today's paper.
Short-sleeved, leaning, one stares
into his cupped hands
lighting a cigarette.
Another shades his eyes and strains
to see across the street.
The third stands like a man
impatient for a bus.

In the present tense of headlines,
they wait all over the world
never knowing what we do:
the cigarette doesn't get lit;
the blinding glare comes from behind;
luck is with the bus.

They have been something
else for hours now, bulldozed
rubble among rubble while the sun

set and moon rose, while the picture
developed and sped over borders,
while the paperboy stuffed inserts
beneath a streetlamp, while I wait
for the coffee, staring at them.

Where Horses Once Were

Once upon a time this really happened.
Four friends went on a picnic.
They packed a basket of usual things,
climbed a nearly rotten fence,
and came to a stream lined with trees,
their roots uncovered by erosion.

They spread a blanket and ate
and watched a few clouds come and go.
They made a game of renaming one
as it changed: basket of flowers, ghost
ship, fish out of water, hornets' nest.
Drowsy with wine and summer they slept.

One woke and listened to birds
twitter about the stream.
He squinted at the orange sun and saw
shadows move over his friends.
Just as a fox disappeared he turned
and saw the tail as it flashed.

He woke the others who said
he dreamed it, and he wasn't sure.
Then two white horses with girls
standing in the stirrups cantered
where the fox had been. All of us
are dreaming the same dream, he answered.

The Interpretation of Waking Life

1.
Unlocked, the back door to dream opens.
A voice like footsteps whispers
There's someone in the house.
I turn toward sounder sleep,
but hands pull me back, Stephanie's
voice shaking: *Eric. Eric wake up listen*
listen someone's in the house.

I refuse and listen
for steps of the furnace lurching on or
joints still adjusting to winter.
By dream glow of night light I hear
nothing, but my breathing

suddenly seizes, catches
at a figure in our doorway fading
toward the baby's room.

2.
No dream yet everything
dreamlike, silent.
I rose and followed.
The hallway was wet, cold.
At Ben's door the figure
stood, motionless,
arms slightly raised.

For an instant it was
a photograph I studied for clues.
I saw a dim hall, at one end
a vaguely human form in a doorframe,
at the other a naked man frozen
in profile, ghostly,
open-mouthed. I couldn't stop

searching it or make it make sense
but I knew it was me

3.
shouting *Hey Hey Hey*
and everything snapped out of place.
The figure turned and
turned into a woman, hair glinting
with snow. Ben jerked awake and wailed.
The woman backed away from me saying *Beth?*
Where's Beth? as I stalked her and Stephanie's
voice behind me said *Ben, Ben* as she
pulled him sobbing from the crib and I pushed
my full weight hard against the woman, forced her
into a chair and stood holding her shoulders,
hissing *What are you doing?*
Why are you here? and I shook her and
I was shaking and I pulled her up, smelled
her drunkenness and dragged her
stumbling through the kitchen through the wide
open door and shoved her out into the darkness.

I bolted the door and went to Ben's room
where Stephanie, colorless, cradled him calm.
Between us in bed he fell asleep quickly.
We stared at the ceiling till dawn, silently
going through it again and again, fixing it,
erasing, imagining worse, wishing
we could go back and lock the door.

By daylight we moved warily,
guilt starting on us for the young
drunk girl who wandered lost into our house
expecting something and someone else,
who could have been beaten or raped or
frozen face down in our yard.
I opened the door and stepped back
from a drift of deep, unpredicted snow.

Wyatt Prunty

A Child's Christmas in Georgia, 1953

Marching through Georgia to bed, he stopped, listened,
And heard, "While shepherds washed their socks by night."
Later, he sang the same skewed line off key,
And his parents howled; until getting it wrong,
He decided, beat getting it right.

But Christmas Eve they read about killing
The first-born, fleeing the land, and returning
By another country, till he couldn't sleep
And had to check so slipped from bed to stare
The darkened height by which the wise men steered.

—Downstairs there were his mother's stacks of albums
And, mantle-high, her unblinking gallery
Of gold-framed gray-beards gazing, and matriarchs
In black, scowling the generations back
Into place; and then there were the others,

His infant older brother who never
Came home, two cousins lost in war, an uncle
Who captained his ship over the flat world's edge,
And one fleece-lined pilot lost years now inside
The stilled weather of a relative's box camera.

And then there were the lines he'd heard in Church,
"Pray that your flight may not be in winter,"
So that was how the pilot disappeared?
And "Woe to the pregnant and nursing," so
That explained his brother, or their mother?

There was one thing he knew by heart by now:
Rubella cooked, cleaned, and scolded her way
Through the house tuning the news and talking back,
Though she didn't vote, and said her baby
Died because he wouldn't come out in Georgia.—

Still standing there and staring up, he pressed
His face till the cold glass fogged and hurt his nose,
Though there was only the street light yellowing
The side yard and his father's dormant garden
And the Talmadges' coiled drive and empty house.

So what were they singing about, the records
And radio? And why all these presents
When over drinks his parents grieved those missing?
What was given if you had to go away
And wound up framed like a silent question?

In the morning Rubella would light the stove;
The paper boy would whistle up Milledge,
Tossing the new day high over one hedge
Into another by the porch for parents
Who ignored their food and read to themselves.

So, still at the window, he studied the sky,
Figuring Pontius Pilate flew for Delta
And that the two parts to the Bible were
The Old and New Estimates, which like Christmas
You read out of the names of those missing.

Falling through the Ice

This, one of our oldest tales—
Late winter and the boy who skates
Ahead in darkness, staying out late

With his thin-voiced friends from school who sail
Over the ice till someone calls them home
And now, turned last, the one drops from sight,
Crying for help where the snow's grained white
Sifts over into dark.

His parents come;
Men ladder out across the ice,
Shouting when they find the hole, but he is gone
Far down below the reasoned town
Where suddenly the shops close twice
Because he's drifting underneath
A surface where his father's breath
Clouds everything but death.
That's how it happens, muted, brief,
And fittingly cold; we tell it over
To ourselves and to each other
Because it pulls us back again
This side of what no man
Has ever laddered over with a name . . .
A riddle, a story, a children's game.

The Lake House

They water-ski over whitecaps
The wind tops up on a man-made lake
Outside Atlanta.

The water widens
Green to blue where their slaloms sculpt
Brief arcs around peninsulas
Jutting out of red-banked Georgia.
It's 1969. She salutes
Left-handed, shading her eyes,
Watching successive skiers pass
And diminish where their wakes fan out;
Then the sun brightens, fixed things waver,

So she turns from her pier and walks into
The cool of a stone summer house.
The skiers crisscross back and forth,
Arms straightened to the ski rope's tug,
Tanned bodies angling back through curve
After curve, rhythmical, as if
Some gradual was silently towing them
Across a plain balanced between
Two bells,
              the earth cupped upward,
The sky cupped down,
                     and water deepening
Blue into blue beyond focus.

Inside, the house stills everything,
Its rooms a series of silences
Arranging furniture, each with
Its view, the lake, a picture window
Squaring another set of silences—
Skiers rounding beyond the window's frame,
Elliptic where they cut high rooster tails
Repeated like a child's toy that's wound,
Released, then wound again.
In the last room down the hall a boy's things
Stand boxed, dated years ago.
                     He's flying now
Over Southeast Asia; what's left behind
Are flags, biplanes, a train, bright cars,
And on the ceiling
              stars arranged
In tiny constellations, Serpens,
Perseus, Andromeda, Orion . . .
Placed in a circle so, "Lights Out,"
He could lie on his back and navigate
Across a ceiling as close and clear
As the luminous face of his father's watch,

His father gone, flying for Nimitz
And Bull Halsey.
                     That ceiling never altered;
Its bright particulars were fixed points of
A boy's departure, small geometries
Set wide against his fear of sleep.
At school he heard the Japanese
Stretched prisoners on bamboo shoots
Then walked away, indelicate
To hear the screams, as the green shafts
Drove up in dark, reaching for light
Till the ground was still and green again.
And then Hiroshima, Nagasaki.
But nothing changed. No one returned.
Beside the cracked, concrete highway to town,
Stone Mountain's half-completed generals
Rode south with Lee, as if the next few steps
Might break them free of their locked origin.
Weekends, the Piedmont Driving Club . . .
Golf, tennis, the pool, or Fox Theater,
and Peachtree Street's dogwoods in bloom—
Then Ponce de Leon Avenue
Unraveling late light through pines,
Curving into 1969
When he's not thought of bamboo shoots
For years, or needed stars fixed overhead
To get to sleep, his missing father
Stalled in shallow spirals,
Wings angling a glide path home
But his Corsair never "touching down."

This is a story about a story,
Two times at once because a woman
Opens her lake house for the summer;
Moving from room to room, she cleans
Windows, gauging her strict horizon

As it distends outside on water,
A litany of successive nows
In which her son and husband stand,
Both young, and thus their lives
Going separately at once, as they
Angle away, two large, high-noon shadows
That never meet.
                    She almost prays,
Saying, "If only for a moment,
Let my thinking take the place
Of their two absences so that
I see them here again, the water
Buoying their energetic waves
As, banking, they ski beyond this lake
Into one bright, continuous curve
Back home, where they dwell again in me."

Their dwelling hollows every room.
Turning, she thinks the sunlight's best
For plants in corners, there urging her ferns
And dieffenbachia up to the clean,
Cool edges of her windowsills
That let onto the water's glaze.
Outside, the lake steadies the day.
Inside, her gaze extends to where
The sky and water meet, a draftsman's line,
The water rising into its opposite.

One opposite confers another.
Sometimes she starts half-stunned because
The skiers lean through curves the way
Her son has learned to shoulder his plane.
She wonders if someway he thinks
He'll find his father out ahead
Caught in one last acrobatic roll
Beneath a Zero tailing him

Like a tireless predatory bird
He cannot see because the sun's
Behind the plane, only a glint
Above before it fires on him
Still in his roll, arching upward
But looking down, two waiting cups,
Two blues identical and wide
Of thought.
              There's nothing up or down,
As their son, one wing away, alert,
Tightens into his own high-speed shedding
That is terror banking into itself.
She is dusting but, seeing this,
Hunches till her hands let go,
Then stares because she's dropped a glass
Between her feet, its tiny fragments
Scattered in a soft blue constellation
Patterning the place she stands, uncertain
What she was doing, or what she will do.
Beyond the house, only the light shatters
Where the wind cuts up the lake like glass
Reflecting upward in a thousand pieces.

The Depression, the War, and Gypsy Rose Lee

> H. L. Mencken called me an ecdysiast. I have also been
> described as deciduous. The French call me a déshabilleuse.
> In less refined circles I'm known as a strip teaser.
> —Gypsy Rose Lee

In a photograph now left to me
Two people lock their arms and pose;
Leaning against a car's black, boxy side,
Cigarettes held out, eyes squinting,
My parents smile into the sun,

So close their white clothes blur
Into one image.
                    It's 1938;
Most things are cheap and unaffordable,
The war ahead with money to spend
And nothing to buy, ready as any
                              substitute
To draft people from part-time jobs
To a full-time hitch,
                    and anonymous
As orders through the mail,
                         or targets
That synchronize with calendars
And newsreels ticking black and white.

Soon things will be standardized,
The prefab buildings, starched uniforms,
Haircuts, and requisitioned tires,
Even the Big Band Sound on radios
Whose dials illuminate the stilled faces
Of those listening for news between
Two coasts darkened against attack.

Traveling west at forty-five,
My parents will drive at night to duck the heat
And save the rationed, recapped tires
That peel their tread regardless what.

Promises.
         All California long.
Belief, an exhausted Chevrolet
With running boards and rings gone bad,
They call it Gypsy Rose Lee because
It's only got the bare essentials . . .
But takes them out answering orders
By traveling nights and sleeping days,

Helps detour them through one dull rental
After another for five years.

Later, an academic life.
They lose one child, have three more,
                              progress,
Until the body's fractions add up
Against its certainties.
                         Sometimes
A radio left on all night
Because the weather's hot and still;
No one can sleep, but no one talks
Either.
           Or a dog barks at a car
Passing too slowly to be going
Anywhere but home, so late
That being late doesn't matter anymore.

Sometimes necessity becomes its own
Dwindling fact, like the stripper's need
For money,
                  whose name they gave their car,
A joke to reconcile them to the things
They wanted then but couldn't have,
Like Kilroy, who only wanted to go home;

And beyond necessity, some hope
For other things put in the names
They gave to their children, to each other,
And the explanations handed their children
Because explaining things becomes
A way of naming them also.

Locked arms to pose a photograph
Surviving all these two survived,
No hint of what they saw ahead

Making them smile
                    except
The camera's implicit place,
Circular and reflecting
Out of its own dark precision,
Dark like the theaters where people sat
Taking in short, censured newsreels
And narrow as the wised-up cold war
That followed,
                    shadowing
The corny jokes on television,
Canned laughter over whiz-bombs, trick ties
With lights blinking across the *fifties,*
One whoopee-cushioned sigh of relief . . .

Like the relief reckoned by Gypsy Rose Lee
Writing her memoirs in 1955,
Addressing them to her son
And counting everything she owned,
Enumerating respectability,
The Rolls with matching luggage, the house
In New York on East Sixty-third
Complete with pool and elevator—
"Some little things removed,
Some big ones gathered up."

One innocence erodes another,
With neither one accurate in what
It pushes forward like a handbill
Or cart loaded with incidentals;
And no one cautions against the little things
Adding up in closets and storage rooms
To another set of incidentals,
Building toward one solemn rummage sale
Held, after the last big fire and funeral,
In everybody's yard,
                    but casual now

As a part-time worker taking orders
Or soldier on temporary duty,
Casual as someone sick
Who is left alone, dozing among
The pastel cards well-wishers have sent . . .

A several and sad innocence,
That spot an audience will watch
When a magic trick takes place,
Distraction made unique yet shared
And similar to the way you tighten
Inwardly to smile or seem natural
When someone takes your picture,
                              the day
Brought down to one approximation,
Leaving each one a little foolish,
Like a naked man whose navel's full of lint.
But in this photograph that's left
To me it's 1938.
                   Everything is
Ahead like something on a map
That someone reads in a car at night,
The road jostling a flashlight so
The map is hard to figure out,
This picture that they leave,
                        the one I find

Which now becomes a photograph I take
Of someone photographing me.
Cameras zoomed into each other,
Two lenses fix on interiors
That stop down to blank shutters cutting
Part to smaller part, like mirrors set
In a barber shop, facing
Their diminishing reflections.

Even diminishment provides
A kind of movement,
                    an always falling,
Like motion sickness,
                    but felt the way
An overloaded plane lifts off
Then doesn't climb but runs for miles
Barely above the trees until
Gathering speed
                    the nose tilts up
And looking back you feel yourself
Dropping away
                    through what you see.

Byron Herbert Reece

Mountain Fiddler

I took my fiddle
That sings and cries
To a hill in the middle
Of Paradise.

I sat at the base
Of a golden stone
In that holy place
To play alone.

I tuned the strings
And began to play,
And a crowd of wings
Were bent my way.

A voice said
Amid the stir:
"We that were dead,
O Fiddler,

"With purest gold
Are robed and shod,
And we behold
The face of God.

"Our halls can show
No thing so rude
As your horsehair bow,
Or your fiddlewood;

"And yet can they
So well entrance
If you but play
Then we must dance!"

Burial of Earth

After the beech was all that held its leaves
Against the wind, against the coming on
Of lessening days when every dusk retrieves
A colder sharpness than day had at dawn,
Suddenly the brooks were under ice,
And their low mumbling proclaimed them lost
Beneath the white and twofold artifice
Forged in the chilly foundry of the frost.
Yet the earth lived beneath its ragged cape
Of leaf and mould until the circled moon
Surrendered up its poor pale borrowed heat
And fled, with its star ally, to escape
The cloud that bore the first snowfall, and soon
Burial of earth and water was complete.

Marry the Moon

Word of it got to his work-bent ear
High on the hill as he cut the trees,
Low in the valley he came to clear
Word of it went like the buzz of bees.
Once he heard it he knew no rest,
Once he knew it he heard no sound
But the wild thing beating within his breast
Like the sexton's tread on graveyard ground.

Log butt, tree top, all he saw
Changed at once to a lovely face
Coveted, courted, held in awe,
Palmed and kissed at the trysting place
Hard by the waters of Clayburn Creek
Deep in the wood that has no name,
Feathery soft on either cheek,
Full on the lips that seared like flame.

Let the lintel fall to the sill,
The rooftree sag and the open sky
Look through the rafters; let the hill
Return to sedge, now green with rye
To gladden the bride that will not look
Far from the window to see it grow;
Forget the footlog to span the brook,
Forget in the spring of the year to sow.

Forget, forget; but tell her this,
O tell her this to cause her pain:
"Because your heart that was mine is his
I never shall darken your door again.
Should any missing me seek in sorrow
Send them down to the pool to seek,
For there I marry the moon tomorrow
At noon of night in Clayburn Creek."

Roads

A pace or two beyond my door
Are highways racing east and west.
I hear their busy traffic roar,
Fleet tourists bound on far behests
And monstrous mastodons of freight
Passing in droves before my gate.

The roads would tow me far away
To cities whose extended pull
They have no choice but to convey;
I name them great and wonderful
And marvels of device and speed,
But all unsuited to my need.

My heart is native to the sky
Where hills that are its only wall
Stand up to judge its boundaries by;
But where from roofs of iron fall
Sheer perpendiculars of steel
On streets that bruise the country heel

My heart's contracted to a stone.
Therefore whatever roads repair
To cities on the plain, my own
Lead upward to the peaks; and there
I feel, pushing my ribs apart,
The wide sky entering my heart.

All the Leaves in the Wildwood

When softly from the shuttered east
The eye of day began to stare
We crossed the fields, and saw the beasts
All lying close together there.
And farther on where trembling lay
The shadows at the feet of day
The fallen vines, the green leaves wist
How she and I with our lips kissed
And lightly went upon our way.

We made no sound at all upon
The green leaves of the forest floor,

And as we walked the brooks that run
Forbade her wade them, so I bore
Her in my arms; and in the mist
The thin green leaves of the wildwood wist
How she and I with our lips kissed
And went on lightly to our door.

We made a cup of the wildwood leaves
And filled it with the water clear,
And where the stone the water cleaves
She drank and I drank after her.
The hushed air made no slightest stir,
And lightly in the morning mist
All the leaves in the wildwood wist
How she and I with our lips kissed
And parted with no more than that.

Alane Rollings

Irma Lee

One weekend when she came home from college
her mother was standing in the front yard
smiling, in sun and a new dress.
Before she left on Sunday,
her mother had given her the dress.
One weekend when she stayed at school
she lost her home, her father, and her mother.
When she did get home, there was only
what was left by the tornado.
She and her sister spent a morning walking through the rubble
in case there was anything to find—
anything small and solid—silverware,
a silver box of money—every woman had one.
Her mother had called her name before she died,
mistaking the woman who'd found her for my mother:
"Irma Lee—"

There were other things about that time
I have been promised to be told sometime.
Sometimes I have an image of my mother
younger, wearing a dress of mine.

To Speak of the World As If There Were No Other

The most persistent principles of the universe are accident and error.

The things that happen are too big for my voice:
catastrophes local and global. Oceans boiling,
mountains lost to rain, volcanic craters
piled with yellow sulphur like the gates to hell.
 We talk of the world as if there were no other.
On this day that began so long ago,
men sought the major secrets in fire, water, earth, and air
and variously found them there. The elements
don't do favors, but they aren't malicious, either;
human forces scare us more.

 It's the unpredictability in things—the way
a butterfly fluttering in Brazil can make a tornado in New Mexico.
The day you set great spaces of sky between us,
the world went mysterious before my eyes.
All I'd ever misunderstood was torn from me
like a little band of birds that had lived so high they were invisible
until they dropped to the earth, dead.
 I made a note in my diary to stand outside in my nightgown
on November 17, 1999, and wait for the meteor shower, some chaos
on a grand scale to bear witness to the general confusion.
There's no end to what I may have lost by then.

 All of nature's alterations make me think of you:
the godlike movement of water; seasons that hesitate to change
and those that change too quickly; the quiet deaths that come with every
    change
and go unnoticed. And the law
of the Eternal Return, which rebuilds continents; which soothes
a billion people in need of a monsoon; which is always bringing
new catastrophes.
 When rehearsing for the end of the world, I should realize
that the elements don't understand me, that it's up to me

to understand the elements, to use my wits to transmit the suspense of life
and love the earth as if either I or it were soon to be no more.

Why is love not returned as specified?
Does it get caught in the winds that push birds off course
and throw them into mountains? I bang my head
against natural deceptions: When I no longer loved you,
I began to love you. I'd fling my arms around anyone
as if we'd just escaped from a catastrophe together.
On this shining, green landscape moving with increasing speed,
there's always a wind in the air, or lost in a fire somewhere.
You who can collapse walls with a deep breath, do you still
expose yourself to it, hoping for pneumonia? Do you wait
for minutes of joy in days of despair? When whirling storms
chase each other across the planet, is all nature saying
you've ceased to be loved? Afraid of drought, flames, floods,
how can you be afraid of me? There's always a fire
in search of a wind. You'll never tire of the sky.

Reasoning with myself, my dreams grow ice-aged.
I drink a glass of curative water, lost in a circular argument:
if one loves, and is loved, the rest should follow.
I gave my heart, you gave it back.
I get disenchanted with nature's majesty.
I try not to look at the sky; it acts up.
Though the trades blow straight and steady in the heavens,
and you were mistaken about me: I'm good at dreaming
disturbed dreams on beautiful, commonplace days,
but I can be happy. You just never saw me like that.
You felt the things I said might drive you mad.
you'd already heard every possible truth about yourself
as if a wind had stripped you of everything and was dissatisfied,
as if I were waking you up to say the world was on fire,
fire, fire and you had no water. I'd be crying so hard
all of creation could hear me, and you'd keep your confusion secret
out of confusion. Did you always have to use force?

The air is heavy and soft. I need
its affection. Grief and love
increase themselves as they wind their way inside me.
    Sealed in the sorrow that outlasts desire,
I find you in the things of the earth
that I accept now without struggle:
the occasional jagged edges of clouds; trees going through
crises; the quiet deaths that come with every change of season.
    On our long pilgrimage of talk, we passed through
freezing rain and temperate warmth. Somewhere else,
with others, we may say that it's for always, as we told
each other, the future landscape oddly like the past.
    In the silence of a planet holding its breath,
I'll still think of you in connection with the open air
and speak of the earth as if there were no other—
a place for the waiting out of things. If we're lucky,
as we follow our fates, the atmosphere will thicken bit by bit
in our wakes, leaving behind us
a train of transparent, evening clouds.

Larry Rubin

The Gift of Time

Within the dimension that lingers, that curves its flight
Like swallows in their season, that rolls about
In globes of dark and light, always returning
The river to its source, the sun to its home
In an older star, something dimly rests,
Perfected like a stillness within time,

A holy center where the flame is not
Consumed. This is the gift of time, the vault
Which holds the core of all that lasts. The girl
Who fled the motions of my arms, my father's
Fear of calendars, the very time
It takes to read a poem—all unravel into

Simple strands of light that feed the flame.
The river changes in its course, the swallow
Nests and dies, the sun descends to spheres
Unknown to earth; yet nothing can be missing
From that frozen pause, the floating eye
Of every storm that paralyzed a clock.

This is the gift of time: dimensions die.

The Alarm

Run for cover when you love; be glad
For silence, caves of steel within the heart—
Hide! The heavy beast roams, it will eat
You, little one, be glad for night. Count
The stars, each a spy; lurk far
From their prying: those hard eyes
Watch to see how far you rise—trust
No one. Trust yourself into your bed,
Pull the coverlets over your head—the beast
Stalks toward your glowing door. Hide
From the craters in his eyes, hide
From the lava in his thighs. Hide.

Instructions for Dying

When they call you from the grave, you must
Swim upward, using a winding stroke.
You must ascend swiftly through dark green
Pressures, before your eardrums burst with the force
Of what is spinning by. If you black out,
Consciousness will return, though spiral swimming
Dizzies the identity. Rise
Toward light with lungs strained to endure
The cries of drowning voices, sirens who pluck
The swimmers from the lonely vortex. Rise
Through shimmering green, past moments of forgetting
Till almost at the surface, one
Last leap toward light, then the final
Layer of foam—and burst out into air,
A child with no name, breathing above
The waters, who never learned to swim.

Bus Terminal

The dispatchers reign from a glass case secured
By height from predestined travelers
Massing, throbbing, dying at the door
Of each messianic bus. Scheduling
Salvation of the ticket-holders (each
Upheld by faith that nothing can go wrong—
Not now that grace is governed by an engine,
A clock, and a loudspeaker), they click off
Cities enroute to New Jerusalem.

Yet the smooth network sometimes jams upon
A storm, a crash, a jolted cam shaft;
Timetables torn, the travelers wait in limbo,
Glancing for assurance to the cage.
But the god has departed from the glass:
The dispatchers move in troubled silence, making
No sign to the ticket-holders, refusing
To suspend the sacraments, going through the motions
That used to make the schedules work.

Bettie Sellers

Charlie Walks the Night

Charlie stalks the night, dark as the painter
silent on the ridge. His bare feet touched cold
leaves with no feeling; his eyes reach only
for the phantoms of his dream. Night after night,
he travels paths never seen by Brasstown's sun.

When he was eight, his mama put the key down deep
inside a pail, sure that water's touch would wake
him gently, send him stumbling back to bed. But,
Charlie took the bucket, poured the water out,
and walked an extra mile. Then Mama tied a string

around his toe, the other end to hers, so she could
wake and keep her boy inside. She felt a little
silly when he turned sixteen, big boy like that,
and him all tied to Mama's toe. Now, Mama's gone,

and Charlie's free to walk. He never knows just
where he's been, up Cedar Ridge, or down by Big
Bald Creek where pools run dark with sleeping
trout—no sign to mark his way except the muddy
footprints on the rough pine porch, and sometimes,
scraps of Oak leaves stuck on quilts that Mama made.

Three Women Named Rebecca

I.
I followed him across Unicoi's Long Trail,
walking tracks of the loaded wagon,
my mother's carved oak bed tied on behind.

In Kirby Cove, I patched quilts,
guarded chickens and children
while he preached through the valleys,
spreading Salvation from his buggy. I hoed
my garden patch, warmed his bed
and cooked his meals when he came home.

It was cold on the slopes. Painter and bear
wandered down to prey on my beehives
and in my hen house. Many's the night
I took the shotgun down from oaken pegs
and fired a volley echoing lonely across
Brasstown and up to Double Knob.

Once, when he had gone toward Gumlog,
the baby sickened and died of summer complaint.
Because of the heat, I buried her myself
and read the Word over the small mound.

II.
After thirty, I had a child. My baby's
blue coverlet lay warm against my robe
with lace falling down the arms.

At eight, he died in Grandmother's bed.
No one understood my guilt; I could not save
him with cold cloths and love.

There was a school picture, blurred
where he squinted his eyes against the light.
I had the blurs enlarged to sit on the mantle.

My last years, I wore my best blue dress
and hat every day, waited rocking on the porch
till it was time to go to his funeral.

III.
From disturbing dreams,
I wake in Great-grandmother's bed,
touch antique oak that knew her birth
to reassure myself that I am real,
the living part of this long line.

Days I keep busy, but nights I relive
two women, one in homespun, one in blue,
searching down hospital corridors
for my children who flowed out like blood,
too small to call by any name.

Two women named Rebecca come at night
to hold my hands. They know: eight years
or two was better than no child at all.

Don't Send Me Off Like Some Three-Legged Dog

In memory of Prof. Adams, who told me tales

John Lowe has gone to join his other leg,
the right one Neighbor Sam cut off with knife
and saw that February day when winds
perverse and raw as March whipped oak limbs

sideways, off from true, crushed nerve and bone
beyond repair. "Don't throw it out!" John groaned.

"Don't let me go to meet my Maker
less than whole. Don't send me off

to hop along the golded streets of Heaven
like some three-legged dog." So Sam devised
a coffin smaller than a child's; of oak
he sawed it, sealed it tight. And, while his stump

was healing, John whittled angels, tall and fair,
with flowing robes, since who knows anyhow
if angels have legs under all that heavenly garb.
The decorated coffin graced the corner

of his room for forty years while John
made do with wooden legs, another carved
when one grew splintery with plowing
rocky mountain cornfields, tending pigs.

And when the neighbors called, or strangers rode
through Brasstown, John would show his coffin,
tell about the fateful day he lost his leg.
He'd tap the lid, smooth angel's hair,

and muse how Peter's holy touch would put
his parts together once he got there,
send him off down shining streets to meet
God man-to-man, as any should. This day,

as it was told, they buried all of John,
coffin within coffin, laid him down to rest
among the oaks that shade the rising slopes
of Double Knob. The preacher, come on horseback

over Unicoi, prayed long and loud
so all could hear, and Peter surely know
what he must do when John and all his legs
comes knocking, knocking at the golden door.

Miracle at Raven Gap

"If I could have a mess of greens
just once before I die."
Old Mary Dean lies pale and thin,
her kinfolk standing by.

"I've got a patch of turnips, Min,
don't guess they'll hurt her none.
I'll fry a pone of cornbread too,
be back here when the sun

sets down in Raven Gap." So Nell
went home and fixed a plate
for Mary Dean's last dying wish—
and with a will she ate.

Next morning, Nell thought ghosts could walk.
She started, gave her head a scratch
when out her window saw at dawn
Old Mary digging in her turnip patch.

Charlie Smith

Omnipotence

I wanted to see the emotion in my brother's face
the night his child was born, I wanted tears, the face
red and beaten and his wife gray and nearly dead
in the ripped sheets and the baby slick
from the gushed oils of the body—I was glad my brother
couldn't take the birth and ran outside
to vomit into the gardenias and the midwife ordered
him to stay there and his wife screamed and choked
and screamed for help and my brother fell to his knees
in the yard praying or crying and the storm whipped
the chinaberries and made the fence wire sing and
the old house thumped and thudded against itself
as the crying and the screaming went on until
dawn when as the gray streaks raised themselves
like Hercules lifting the night off I saw
the ground littered with blue flowers and my brother
soaked to the skin slumped against the side of the house
while the midwife, tense on the steps, looked down at him
holding herself in bloody arms apologizing.

The Sweetness of a Peach

1
Somebody must have rummaged in these attic boxes
recently, among the masks and dried petticoats, the refolded
telegrams begging on relentlessly for money

and love. My mother dreamed from here she saw a hundred babies
lying white and naked on the moonlit lawn. 'At first
I thought they were mushrooms,' she said, as if the important fact
was that she recognized them at all. My father, sleep swimmer,
pulled the clear waters of his death around him. 'Fatal priest,
come at last' was among the phrases drifting
down these attic stairs. Here we put on plays;
children taught each other's flesh: prick
and cunt: be gentle when you touch. We flew the hundred flags
an uncle bought us, from all the disappeared empires of the world:
Thebes and Rome, Persia and the Confederacy—countries
that haunted us like aches along the bone. My sister found a snake skin
coiled between two boxes containing our grandmother's diaries
and our mother's soiled summer dresses.

2
The floor is painted blue.
Above it windows let down a graceful light. The longest, I think,
lifetime ago, I constructed a fortress up here
that would protect me: stacks
of *Atlantic Monthly* magazines, the red square boxes of my mother's
former circus duds, my father's horse chains. In the cracks
I mortared in my dreams, all those harlequins
dressed for tropical weather, patriots
of the nighttime country who would never, they swore,
be rounded up. I could be saved then, my sisters too,
their barely explainable bodies moving
among the trees of light. Years later my best friend
fell back across the bed crying, 'Why

am I such a coward?' having reached a place
he could not return from whole. And yet he still lives,
as I live, on my feet in this
Demilitarized Zone, where the generations gather,
pretending they are ghosts.
                    Blue dahlia, iris, the sweet

unenduring delicacy of a daffodil. Look how the world
can turn around: set a single yellow daffodil
in a white vase. Place the vase on a pinewood table
in the light. Step back and spend the next hundred years
staring it down.

3

In a diary dated August 12, 1893, my grandmother wrote:
'I have seen him walking on the road
when there was no one there, and I cannot understand
how I smell the scent of tea olive, I feel the red dust
on my wrist, I taste the sweetness of a peach,
and he is nothing.'
Grown old, she traveled from town to town
carrying, like an antique brooch, the faint
and singular hope that he might be living there,
unnoticed and uncared for
among the rise and fall of other people's lives.

Jehovah's Witness

Flying into myself is the image, specific
though peripheral, cakewalk of the mind
as the leaves rush down to join the earth.

Someone has just come back from Arabia
where he was jailed for drinking wine.

On the Negev three sisters draw water
from the only well for a hundred miles.
Under such conditions a thousand years of God
become a cup of water held to the lips.

The wind will eventually make a human sound
if you listen long enough. As will everything else.

I think of the banana trees growing by the station house
in Barwick, Georgia, two hundred miles off their range.
As far as I am concerned they prove the existence of God.

And the old woman who was once my mother
takes a sip of wine and thinks and thinks.
It has never happened like this before, she says.
I stand at the window watching the wind gash the rain
and wonder, What—death? winter come so early? the revolution's
blue flags? and then I figure it's nothing

nothing has ever happened like this before.

What Can Be United

I speak directly of religion now, of the
hogback preachers bending over frail women
in white churches; I have leaned off my bench
to catch a glimpse of the verifiable light needling
from their crimped fingers;
                              I have waked early in that time of night
when the day is a prophecy
and gone out to walk in the stream. I feel the fugitive, yearling fishes,
backed into pools, feathering my ankles, and I reach up
to grope down handfuls of starry leaves, having decided
there is a goddess after all, some dimension
of beauty or possession behind the raging
face of the woman evangelist
in the town square. Yesterday my brother

climbed the rough-hewn hill behind our house
and sat for six hours on an outcropping of battered stone.
This evening, when the night accelerates, he will tell me how he marked
the last red splashes
of elderberry and oak, he will say the names of trees

that were once passwords
into the other world. He thinks the earth
has lost itself in dreams, he says we must find the
mystery of our lives in the dust of our forefathers' bones,
he says, *winter wheat, columbine,*
loosestrife, solomon's seal, he prepares his body
for a journey that will leave it behind.
                                    I thought this morning,
as I emptied my pockets for the crumpled man
who called to me from the sidewalk
for passage to Spartanburg, I thought
there must be a simple way to untie the strangeness of all things,
there must be a turning of the body
in which, as the flex of muscles lifting toward the
few syllables we can repeat without misery commences,
we can at last be united. I thought we can turn
to our murderers with praise
because we are finally too tired even for resistance,
even for righteousness. Someone said, speaking to me
from bushes beside the road, *Here*
is your brother, but when I turned
there was no one there.

My father gave money to the poor all his life. On Christmas
he lined them in awkward fugitive rows
on the front lawn and passed out hams
and turkeys and boxes of clothes for the children.
To each husband he gave a bullet
for the truth that was in it, to each wife he gave
a book of blank pages, and to the ones without
kin, he gave radios—he made us all,
family and poor, wear white flowers in our hair, he made us dance
to songs of his devising, he passed among us
offering sweet drinks and words of encouragement
laced with derision
and blame. He made speeches all afternoon, complaining
about the government, pointing his finger like a gun

at this one and that one, forcing us to kneel
and pray with him his high sordid prayer
that God would bring down the rain of lingering madness
on all his enemies. Eventually we were clapping and singing, we
were dancing, on a power of our own, casting looks
at the dew in the pine trees, at each other's throats, which, raised
in the obsessive gulping mechanics of our song,
were white and bare.

Passage

1

What you gave to me along with scarlet
gilia and Cherokee rose, that afternoon in Georgia,
in the backyard where the flowers,
bold as Zouaves, had taken the ground back,
was the simple knowledge
of continuance, the world's message of recurrence
and display, as, on a remarkable morning
thirty-five years ago, my mother showed me the angel
blossoming out of lines and flesh
in her palm. I mean, what I make up
I must learn to live with,
and it is always ongoing.

                    A man,
breaking down in a bus station,
races down steps to speak one last time
to his child, to hold the sweet-smelling
head against his body once more before leaving forever.
          And the child, in a dream,
will see a man standing naked on the green bank of a river
and will know him as the one stranger
his heart longs for; and the face that slowly turns toward him
will be a face of such whiteness

that he remembers the camellias blooming
under the windows of the house he was born in,
the house he was taken from one winter night
when the world creaked in its passage, bundled
and weeping carried to the car and away.

2
I would like to have at least one secret
I could carry hidden on my person
the way my father carried in his pocket
the small gray stone
he picked up when he was ten
from the banks of the Eno River
in North Carolina. I would wait for the time
when, despairing or exuberant, years
later, I would draw it forth
and you would look at it and say yes, yes I know,
I carry it too.

3
A bass, disturbed by footsteps,
descends, leaving casual rings
on the surface of the pond. The surface is pricked
by gnats and mayflies
so it looks as if invisible,
unfelt rain, apparent only
at the moment of union,
is falling. Water returning to water
is what it might be, though
it is not. So the emptiness
of the last house we lived in
repeats itself
in another version, is transformed
by the delicate and
relentless process of memory
into a white ship sailing
on a green sea.

4

Your hands open on my chest, press
me back into roiled sheets; outside
it is spring and the flowers of blue phlox
and amaryllis lie on the grass
after rain. We hear the creak of the chain
as someone draws water from the well
and you are telling me a story
I have heard ten thousand times,
about your father, about
how he turned once at the bottom of the drive
to wave his gray hat
before disappearing forever. These are lies,
I know, elaborate and sustained,
neither desperate nor sordid, stories
that become more beautiful
in the telling. You chant the names of the missing
over and over, undisturbed
by their passing, and it is as if the well chain
is drawing not water
but the world itself, the mystery, attached
and flowing, the moment by moment
particularity of being, passed
from hand to hand, cool and clear,
unknowable and known, phrase
and touch, permanent only
because ongoing.

Ron Smith

Water Tower

The wind behind us pulled on our packs.
Hands firmly on each steel rod, we were careful
to show we were never careful, even when
the ladder left the huge bolted leg to lean
for the catwalk circling above us like Saturn's rings.
A hundred feet above the streetlight
we unloaded blankets, bananas, and rum crooks.

Clenching our teeth on sweet tobacco,
we thought we had left town already.
Our dark neighborhoods at our feet,
the black sky strewn with close blue stars,
we matched nickels on the very top
and pulsed wholly red with warning
to pilots they were still too near the earth.

Our parents thought we hugged the ground
in the gnat-buzzing woods.
But even mosquitoes couldn't reach us up there.
Police Chief Crowder moved below us
in his slow square car, prowling the streets' angles,
throwing his yellow beam into the usual darkness,
behind the Webbers' cinder block garage, under
the Methodist preacher's hedges.

We slept on the catwalk along the curve of steel,
and seven of us, toe to head,
could surround the whole town's water.
We rose full of water in the dawn, shivering,

hanging long pisses to the familiar street,
trembling stiffly, quickly down the cold rungs,
while dogs harangued the milkman,
and the big trucks over on 17
made their hollow sounds passing through.

　　　—for Stan

Leaving Forever

My son can look me level in the eyes now,
and does, hard, when I tell him he cannot watch
chainsaw murders at the midnight movie,
that he must bend his mind to Biology,
under this roof, in the clear light of a Tensor lamp.
Outside, his friends throb with horsepower
under the moon.

　　　　　　He stands close, milk sour
on his breath, gauging the heat of my conviction,
eye-whites pink from his new contacts.
He can see me better than before. And I can see
myself in those insolent eyes, mostly head
in the pupil's curve, closed in by the contours
of his unwrinkled flesh.

　　　　　　At the window he waves
a thin arm and his buddies squall away in a glare
of tail lights. I reach out my hand to his shoulder,
but he shrugs free and shows me my father's narrow eyes,
the trembling hand at my throat, the hard wall
at the back of my skull, the raised fist framed
in the bedroom window I had climbed through
at 3 A.M.

"If you hit me, I'll leave forever,"
I said. But everything was fine in a few days, fine.
"I would have come back," I said, "false teeth and all."
Now, twice a year after the long drive, in the yellow light
of the front porch, I breathe in my father's whiskey,
ask for a shot, and see myself distorted in
his thick glasses, the two of us grinning,
as he holds me with both hands at arm's length.

Declaiming

When my father takes my poems
in his flight-broken hands,
he holds my few words
at arm's length,
raises his rich, unused voice,
and calls each syllable
so carefully you can see
him declaiming Bryant
fifty years ago, at attention
beside his lunch pail
in the single room of Stilson School.

There, his cheeks are full of blood,
and he is handsome.
Parris Island is two years north.
He smells like the cows he milked
in the early Georgia dark.
He moves down each row
of phrases with the grimness
of those who feel
they must make the earth yield
its sweet corn,
its crouching Japanese,

catching up against
hard roots, going on

up the burning islands of the Pacific,
peering into the flaring dark
of each step north.
Against beachhead sunsets he sees
the Zeros sputter and go down.
In foxhole after foxhole he dreams
of dusty fields where he falls
behind the mule
and the rows close over him
and he comes up changed,
atabrine yellow,
wavering in the merest breeze,
his body whispering.

The days have gathered
into straight lines behind him.
After half a century
of the silent heft of steel
he is left again with a handful
of someone else's words,
words that slip
between the thick, crooked fingers
like the lightest of seeds.

Leon Stokesbury

An Inkling

Just two weeks graduated from Central High
in 1942, my mother finds herself
employed as the candy girl
at the State Theatre
in downtown Oklahoma City.
                              And just
across the street, at the Liberty Theatre,
my father, who does not know
my mother yet, is head usher,
although Assistant Manager
is his actual title,
as he is quick to tell.

From where she stands, my mother
sometimes gazes across the street
and sees my father taking tickets,
sweeping, changing the marquee.

He really is a pretty boy,
she thinks. And she
is not alone. All the usherettes
at the State think so too.
And they have all, all that are
in the game anyway, given him
a shot, a little wiggle, the once-over,
the come-on, these last few weeks,
to no avail. Why is that?
My mother does not know.

There is a war on, and there
are Army and Navy boys
everywhere, half of them not much
or no older than herself,
but god, doesn't he look divine
in that navy-blue head usher's uniform,
with gold braid up and down
each arm and pants leg too,
and gold buttons, and epaulets
with gold fringe hanging off.

She thinks how fine they both
might look together on a date,
but her State uniform
is green, pool-table-green,
with dark green braid
and buttons too.
                Even so,
she loves it. The pants
and jacket make her think
of Dr. Dolittle.
                She remembers
reading Dr. Dolittle back
ten years before. Her favorite book
had been *Dr. Dolittle and the Secret Lake*
because it was so thick.
It made her blush
when people came up
and remarked how smart
she must be to read
such a big book.
So she read it four times.

But she remembers also
the picture on the cover
with Dr. Dolittle in his pool-

table-green jacket and trousers,
or were they called pantaloons?
She cannot recall.

And then, one week later,
Charlene is out front, and she says
something to my father, and he says
something back, and he smiles.
And when my mother,
from behind the candy counter
and the tinted plate-glass doors,
sees that smile,
that settles things.

Something in that smile.
                              So
by mid-July she has dropped
her crumbs, she has stood
upwind, she has cast her line,
and he has bit the bait, her hook
now nestled tight against
the inside of his lower lip,
and she is seriously
considering hauling him in.

On their third date he borrows a car,
and after work they go
to Beverly's Drive-In and order
Chicken-in-the-Rough. She spent
weekends and holidays the year before
as a carhop there: Beverly's
is perfect. Beverly's is A-OK.
Beverly's is divine.

Then she shows him a place
out by Indian Stadium
where they can park

and spend some time alone.
They have not worn
their uniforms, and she is glad
she had not asked him to.
                        They stop
at the far end of the stadium
parking lot. The moonlight
shining on the gravel gray
has turned it the color of mercury.
My father turns, and puts his arm
around my mother, and kisses her,
and then he looks down,
and lifts his other hand,
and rests it gently, Oh
so gently, against my mother's
blouse.
            He then applies
a small amount of pressure.
He wants her to see that
he is kind, but firm.
                        And so,
gently, he applies pressure
to her blouse, and thus
to the bra beneath that blouse,
and, thus, to the breast
beneath that bra.
                        And he looks down
into her eyes, questioning. Hesitant,
but firm.
                        And my mother looks
up into the glow and darkness
and sees that question there.
An omen, maybe. An inkling.
And it makes her think, for just
an instant, of her own father, Clyde,
four years back.
                        Clyde had never

questioned, had he? Oh no.
That bourbon-breath on top of her,
that ape-like pawing,
pushing her down, the reek
and stink of whiskey over
everything, and the stumbling off
afterward, off her bed and out
into the kitchen to vomit and pass out
like the pig he was.
                        The next day,
her Mama took her on the bus
eighty-five miles from Weatherford
to Oklahoma City and the good
open arms and home of Aunt Helen.
But then her Mama rode right back
to Weatherford and stayed.
For more than one whole year
she stayed—until Clyde beat
her up and ran off one last time.

So my mother lifts her eyes
and sees that questioning. She notices,
too, a tiny band of platinum—
perspiration—above my father's lip,
for, although it is past midnight,
it stays hot in Oklahoma City
in the summertime.
                        In ten months
my father will be sweating more
with a fever of one hundred and five,
having contracted malaria
on the island of New Guinea,
soon to be sent stateside
as his only cure.
                        But now my mother
gazes up at my father's eyes.
I tell you she looks up,

and she sees what is in
my father's eyes, and what
will be in my father's eyes,
and what will never be
in my father's eyes, this once
and future moralist wanting
always to do good, to strive,
to find. This pretty boy.

She drops her gaze again
to see the moon's milk spilt
all down the front of her blouse,
and all over my father's hand
resting, firmly, there.
Then she rests her own hand
on the steering wheel, shifts
slightly, and leans her heavy head
against my father's shoulder.
As she does so, she can feel
the taut muscles along the back
of her neck begin to ease.

She shivers for a second,
then meets his eyes, those obscure
agents of augury, once more.
He is smiling. Such
a gentle face, with such
a gentle smile. And so
she smiles back at him.
And it is in this fashion,
with all the world at war,
that my mother smiles back,
to let my father know that
this will do. This is
satisfactory. This little sphere
inside this Ford at one end
of this empty parking lot

will do for her, she seems
to say, as she glances down again,
with the whole world swirled
in shades of pearl and mercury,
at her breast laved in moonlight,
at my father's hand resting there,
questioning. And it is thus
that she cedes to him,
as though through a scrim
of reverie, that small concession.

John Stone

He Makes a House Call

Six, seven years ago
when you began to begin to faint
I painted your leg with iodine

threaded the artery
with the needle and then the tube
pumped your heart with dye enough

to see the valve
almost closed with stone.
We were both under pressure.

Today, in your garden,
kneeling under the sticky fig tree
for tomatoes

I keep remembering your blood.
Seven, it was. I was just
beginning to learn the heart

inside out.
Afterward, your surgery
and the precise valve of steel

and plastic that still pops and clicks
inside like a ping-pong ball.
I should try

chewing tobacco sometimes
if only to see how it tastes.
There is a trace of it at the corner

of your leathery smile
which insists that I see inside
the house: someone named Bill I'm supposed

to know; the royal plastic soldier
whose body fills with whiskey
and marches on a music box

How Dry I Am;
the illuminated 3-D Christ who turns
into Mary from different angles;

the watery basement,
the pills you take, the ivy
that may grow around the ceiling

if it must. Here, you
are in charge — of figs, beans,
tomatoes, life.

At the hospital, a thousand times
I have heard your heart valve open, close.
I know how clumsy it is.

But health is whatever works
and for as long. I keep thinking
of seven years without a faint

on my way to the car
loaded with vegetables
I keep thinking of seven years ago

when you bled in my hands like a saint.

Losing a Voice in Summer

How many parts rumble it was
how much gravel
dark, light
I don't remember

and it won't echo for me
from the shower stall

though sometimes off the porch
calling my own sons for supper
I can almost

almost hear it

as if you had let it go
out of the corner
of your mouth
like a ventriloquist
without a dummy.

I have no recording

otherwise I would play you
in the shower, repeat you
off the porch

from the cat-walk
of the glass factory have you sing
Go Down Moses
over and over and

tonight
with the reluctant sentence
deep in my head at the hoarsest hour,
dumb and laryngitic and alone

I first understood
how completely I have lost your voice,
father, along with my own.

The Truck

I was coming back from
wherever I'd been when
I saw the truck and
the sign on the back repeated
on the side to be certain
you knew it was no mistake

PROGRESS CASKETS

ARTHUR ILLINOIS

Now folks have different
thoughts it's true about
death but in general it's
not like any race for
example you ever ran
everyone wanting to come in

last and all   And I admit
a business has to have a good
name   No one knows better
than I the value of a good
name   A name is what sells
the product in the first

and in the final place
All this time the Interstate
was leading me into Atlanta
and I was following the sign

and the truck was heavier
climbing the hill than

going down which is as
it should be   What I really
wanted to see was the driver
up close maybe talk to him
find out his usual run
so I could keep off it

Not that I'm superstitious   It's just
the way I was raised   A casket
may be Progress up in Arthur
but it's thought of
down here
as a setback.

Whittling: The Last Class

What has been written
about whittling
is not true

most of it

It is the discovery
that keeps
the fingers moving

not idleness

but the knife looking for
the right plane
that will let the secret out

Whittling is no pastime

he says
who has been whittling
in spare minutes at the wood

of his life for forty years

Three rules he thinks
have helped
Make small cuts

In this way

you may be able to stop before
what was to be an arm
has to be something else

Always whittle away from yourself

and toward something.
For God's sake
and your own
know when to stop

Whittling is the best example
I know of what most
may happen when

least expected

bad or good
Hurry before
angina comes like a pair of pliers

over your left shoulder

There is plenty of wood
for everyone
and you

Go ahead now

May you find
in the waiting wood
rough   unspoken

what is true

or
nearly true
or

true enough.

Jean Toomer

Portrait in Georgia

Hair—braided chestnut,
   coiled like a lyncher's rope,
Eyes—fagots,
Lips—old scars, or the first red blisters,
Breath—the last sweet scent of cane,
And her slim body, white as the ash
   of black flesh after flame.

Georgia Dusk

The sky, lazily disdaining to pursue
   The setting sun, too indolent to hold
   A lengthened tournament for flashing gold,
Passively darkens for night's barbecue,

A feast of moon and men and barking hounds,
   An orgy for some genius of the South
   With blood-hot eyes and cane-lipped scented mouth,
Surprised in making folk-songs from soul sounds.

The sawmill blows its whistle, buzz-saws stop,
   And silence breaks the bud of knoll and hill,
   Soft settling pollen where plowed lands fulfill
Their early promise of a bumper crop.

Smoke from the pyramidal sawdust pile
   Curls up, blue ghosts of trees, tarrying low

Where only chips and stumps are left to show
The solid proof of former domicile.

Meanwhile, the men, with vestiges of pomp,
    Race memories of king and caravan,
    High-priests, an ostrich, and a juju-man,
Go singing through the footpaths of the swamp.

Their voices rise . . the pine trees are guitars,
    Strumming, pine-needles fall like sheets of rain . .
    Their voices rise . . the chorus of the cane
Is caroling a vesper to the stars. .

O singers, resinous and soft your songs
    Above the sacred whisper of the pines,
    Give virgin lips to cornfield concubines,
Bring dreams of Christ to dusky cane-lipped throngs.

Cotton Song

Come, brother, come. Lets lift it;
Come now, hewit! roll away!
Shackles fall upon the Judgment Day
But lets not wait for it.

God's body's got a soul,
Bodies like to roll the soul,
Cant blame God if we dont roll,
Come, brother, roll, roll!

Cotton bales are the fleecy way
Weary sinner's bare feet trod,
Softly, softly to the throne of God,
"We aint agwine t wait until th Judgment Day!

Nassur; nassur,
Hump.
Eoho, eoho, roll away!
We aint agwine t wait until th Judgment Day!"

God's body's got a soul,
Bodies like to roll the soul,
Cant blame God if we dont roll,
Come, brother, roll, roll!

Alice Walker

Part v from "Once"

It is true—
I've always loved
the daring
        ones
Like the black young
man
Who tried
to crash
All barriers
at once,
    wanted to
swim
At a white
beach (in Alabama)
Nude.

Burial

i
They have fenced in the dirt road
that once led to Wards Chapel
A.M.E. church,
and cows graze
among the stones that
mark my family's graves.
The massive oak is gone

from out the church yard,
but the giant space is left
unfilled;
despite the two-lane blacktop
that slides across
the old, unalterable
roots.

ii

Today I bring my own child here;
to this place where my father's
grandmother rests undisturbed
beneath the Georgia sun,
above her the neatstepping hooves
of cattle.
Here the graves soon grow back into the land.
Have been known to sink. To drop open without
warning. To cover themselves with wild ivy,
blackberries. Bittersweet and sage.
No one knows why. No one asks.
When Burning Off Day comes, as it does
some years,
the graves are haphazardly cleared and snakes
hacked to death and burned sizzling
in the brush. . . . The odor of smoke, oak
leaves, honeysuckle.
Forgetful of geographic resolutions as birds,
the farflung young fly South to bury
the old dead.

iii

The old women move quietly up
and touch Sis Rachel's face.
"Tell Jesus I'm coming," they say.
"Tell him I ain't goin' to *be*
long."

My grandfather turns his creaking head
away from the lavender box.
He does not cry. But looks afraid.
For years he called her "Woman";
shortened over the decades to
"'Oman."
On the cut stone for "'Oman's" grave
he did not notice
they had misspelled her name.
(The stone reads *Racher Walker*—not "Rachel"—
Loving Wife, Devoted Mother?)

iv

As a young woman, who had known her? Tripping
eagerly, "loving wife," to my grandfather's
bed. Not pretty, but serviceable. A hard
worker, with rough, moist hands. Her own two
babies dead before she came.
Came to seven children.
To aprons and sweat.
Came to quiltmaking.
Came to canning and vegetable gardens
big as fields.
Came to fields to plow.
Cotton to chop.
Potatoes to dig.
Came to multiple measles, chickenpox,
and croup.
Came to water from springs.
Came to leaning houses one story high.
Came to rivalries. Saturday night battles.
Came to straightened hair, Noxzema, and
feet washing at the Hardshell Baptist church.
Came to zinnias around the woodpile.
Came to grandchildren not of her blood

whom she taught to dip snuff without
sneezing.

Came to death blank, forgetful of it all.

When he called her "'Oman" she no longer
listened. Or heard, or knew, or felt.

v
It is not until I see my first grade teacher
review her body that I cry.
Not for the dead, but for the gray in my
first grade teacher's hair. For memories
of before I was born, when teacher and
grandmother loved each other; and later
above the ducks made of soap and the orange-
legged chicks Miss Reynolds drew over
my own small hand
on paper with wide blue lines.

vi
Not for the dead, but for memories. None of
them sad. But seen from the angle of her
death.

Eagle Rock

In the town where I was born
There is a mound
Some eight feet high
That from the ground
Seems piled up stones
In Georgia
Insignificant.

But from above
The lookout tower
Floor
An eagle widespread
In solid gravel
Stone
Takes shape
Below;

The Cherokees raised it
Long ago
Before westward journeys
In the snow
Before the
National Policy slew
Long before Columbus knew.

I used to stop and
Linger there
Within the cleanswept tower stair
Rock Eagle pinesounds
Rush of stillness
Lifting up my hair.

Pinned to the earth
The eagle endures
The Cherokees are gone
The people come on tours.
And on surrounding National
Forest lakes the air rings
With cries
The silenced make.

Wearing cameras
They never hear
But relive their victory
Every year

And take it home
With them.
Young Future Farmers
As paleface warriors
Grub
Live off the land

Pretend Indian, therefore
Man,
Can envision a lake
But never a flood
On earth
So cleanly scrubbed
Of blood:
They come before the rock
Jolly conquerors.

They do not know the rock
They love
Lives and is bound
To bide its time
To wrap its stony wings
Around
The innocent eager 4-H Club.

"*Good Night, Willie Lee, I'll See You in the Morning*"

Looking down into my father's
dead face
for the last time
my mother said without
tears, without smiles
without regrets
but with *civility*
"Good night, Willie Lee, I'll see you

in the morning."
And it was then I knew that the healing
of all our wounds
is forgiveness
that permits a promise
of our return
at the end.

A Woman Is Not a Potted Plant

her roots bound
to the confines
of her house

a woman is not
a potted plant
her leaves trimmed
to the contours
of her sex

a woman is not
a potted plant
her branches
espaliered
against the fences
of her race
her country
her mother
her man

her trained blossom
turning
this way
& that

to follow
the sun
of whoever feeds
and waters
her

a woman
is wilderness
unbounded
holding the future
between each breath
walking the earth
only because
she is free
and not creepervine
or tree.

Nor even honeysuckle
or bee.

Philip Lee Williams

The Confederate Cemetery in Madison, Georgia

We still plant corn, Edward, green stalks
that squeak and spread to sun
then swell upon your father's grave.
Your first name is all they had
to crack upon the marble's face,
not the sickbed's agony, the feeling
when the ball broke off your leg
and made you kneel when Atlanta
turned to flame and storm.
I do not believe in the resurrection
of your body, Edward. The shade
of water oaks, the sound of clear wind
will hold you down. Your fellows
have no names, only cool marble
slabs and the single word, unknown.
You could bring their pulses back
to me, country boys who spilled life
casually for another useless fight,
for the wreck of thunder on cloudless days,
having won their peace, this shade
of oaks, this victory of silence here
with your single word. You could
stand and tell us what you won,
how passion even stole your name.

Berry Picking

My God, the quicksilver tang of blackberries,
odors of vine and earth—they came back
today, miles and years away. I could
have been bleeding juice from sugared lips,
eight years old and summer darkened,
but I was thirty-six, and winter still
lingered. We would find them, Mark and I,
great coils hung plump with dark blue berries.
We would pick a hatful, eat until our mouths
were royal purple, sweetness lingering,
then dance in our Keds among sunny fields.
I would touch each sunstroked facet
of blackberries as I ate, laughing my way home.
The last time I hunted for berries
I was a boy aching for age and wisdom.
Now I sing for dense thickets
and the swelling seeds as I held them then,
dark upon my palm, then sweetness.

Walking the Dogs with Megan

Step by step I am getting older
Along the paths by Wildcat Creek.
Four dew-spangled spider webs
Bulge from a steady northern wind.
Contessa, you are out on point
This morning, poking up shelf fungi.
A routine succession of hardwoods
Has preceded us, beech and oak
After pine, polk, and blackberry.
You find the first tracks in sand,
A doe and her fawn, two raccoons,

Us from a few days back. I mean
To teach you something by this,
Patience, the spatial distribution
Of pot sherds, woodpecker habitats.
Or nothing. The tracks by the creek
Are from ghost feet, ridge-dreamers.
They do not believe in us,
Crazy bipedal monsters stumbling along
On trails, our woolen beasts in tow.
You, Contessa, leave prints here, too,
Examined in the darkness by creatures
Who confer and agree you are
Essentially innocent, that I am
The image of their legends.
No matter. We share this damp eucharist
Of summer air, and I am quite sad
To know that when night arrives
I will be lost to you, my love,
But not in these woods, and not forever.

In Memory of Raymond Andrews

(1934–1991)

1.

Our restless country shifts in its ice,
Old friend. A January once more holds
Me near the fires where black cats roll
Up and over for a stretch. I bless
That idleness and the letters of your name,
Sink in dreams to your cool reef,
Then rise against it. That laughter
Has me waiting, for you might come here
Once more with beer and magazines
To my front door, all shades of delight.

2.

I shook your soft hand that June
Near Madison Square Garden. You wanted
To spring for Irish coffee, but I left
You and went up in the Penta twelve floors
To bed. We might have gone back
To O'Reilly's, as we did years before,
And drunk all night. You slipped
Past me down that last sidewalk,
Rolling gait, no capacity for enduring
The brotherhood of our failures, tired
Beyond the traffic and the tearing light.

3.

I want to bless that turning away,
Its fatal separation, shake milkweed
To stir our country alchemy; thaw
The night back and go from there.
I want you to sponge that last meal
Off Margaret, have you lead the crew
From Maria's south down the sidewalk,
Ray. I want to change my mind now.
I will go with you for Irish coffee
And chart our Southern lives toward home.

4.

All that last night you wrote notes
For the disposition of your manuscripts, books,
When autumn had come gold and red
Back to Georgia. You took the weave of age,
Spread that uneven tapestry half across
Your house in the woods. You came
Past old lapses, memories of baseball,
Funny-papers stories from the Thirties
When you and Benny were only boys
In Madison. I consecrate all the layers
Of that last long evening before us.

5.

You came back South for that end.
Half of your life in the city, never stopped
To drive, arrived here broken up
And lost to us by bus that season.
I did not dream a solid darkness
Had brought you home. The fresh words
Gone, wild ache of new books faded
To your shelves. I did not dream all
The blank stares had come for you;
The quiet distance had come for you.

6.

You went to the gazebo. The pistol
Had the mass of stars. Words came.
You were sick then, tired, innocent
For your life of hurting anyone, anything.
You spoke to that clear pain. Night
Had come soft and cool, and each star
Held down that black and ending sky.
You held the pistol up and fired.
The shaken earth swayed close.

7.

And now another winter, two years after
You fell. A cold rain rests on Georgia,
Sliding from the thicker oak trunks to moss
And the red earth and a bed of leaves.
There is no resurrection of your body here
Today. Your ashes and their molecules
Spin somewhere near me, and I remain
Alive and broken, or not, as the day permits.
My daughter you never met sips milk
By the January fire and calls to me.

8.

I praise the artlessness of your life,
Ray, that spring in your step, how
As you drank everyone around you grew
Steadily more wonderful. I praise old films
And the Brooklyn Dodgers, your command
Of trivia, genuine risk of real affection.
I praise memory and age and wisdom
for my own purposes, my other life.

9.

Listen to me, Ray: my anger has gone,
But it took my breath to drive past
Your unexpected act. I want to say
I live in your memory, but all sure
Things break down to light and ashes.
I want to say your voice endures
In my hands, that I am your witness
Against this life, that in my quiet days
I hear your deep laughter outside
My front door somewhere toward morning.

Biographical Sketches

Conrad Aiken (1889–1973), although a native of Savannah, Georgia, where he lived until the age of eleven, was born of New Englander parents, and he considered himself a New Englander as well. He moved to Massachusetts in 1901 to live with an aunt after his parents' murder-suicide. At Harvard, his classmates included Heywood Broun, Walter Lippman, Van Wyck Brooks, and T. S. Eliot, to whom he gave his poems for criticism. Aiken wrote more than fifty books of fiction, poetry, criticism, drama, and autobiography. The volume and the difficulty of his work may account for its relative neglect by critics and readers. Nonetheless, he was a significant figure on the modern American literary scene. In 1930 he won the Pulitzer Prize for his *Selected Poems* (1929), while his *Collected Poems* (1953) earned the National Book Award in 1954. He was the consultant in poetry for the Library of Congress in 1950–51 and recipient of the Bollingen Prize in Poetry in 1956, the Academy of American Poetry Fellowship in 1957, the Gold Medal of the National Institute of Arts and Letters in 1958, and the National Medal of Literature in 1969. During the last years of his life he passed his summers in Cape Cod, Massachusetts, and his winters in Savannah. Governor Jimmy Carter named him Georgia Poet Laureate in 1973. Important works include the novels *Blue Voyage* (1927), *Great Circle* (1933), *King Coffin* (1935), *A Heart for the Gods of Mexico* (1939), and *Conversation; or, Pilgrim's Progress* (1940); the poetry books *The Coming Forth of Osiris Jones* (1931), *Preludes for Memnon* (1931), and *Time in the Rock: Preludes to Definition* (1936); and such other works as *Ushant* (1952) and *The Short Stories of Conrad Aiken* (1950).

Coleman Barks (1937–   ) is a native of Chattanooga, Tennessee. He studied at the University of California, Berkeley, and at the University of North Carolina, where he earned his Ph.D. He taught in the University of Georgia English and creative writing programs from 1967 to 1997. His books of poetry include *The Juice* (1972), *New Words* (1974), *We're Laughing at the Damage* (1977), and *Gourd Seed* (1993). Since the late 1970s his translations of the Persian mystic poet Rumi have earned him international recognition and have been anthologized in the *Norton Anthology of World Masterpieces*. In 1995 his collected translations were published by HarperCollins in San Francisco as *The Essential Rumi*, which became a best-seller—a rare occurrence for a volume of poetry. *The Illuminated Rumi* followed in 1997. Barks has been widely anthologized and published. He is the recipient of the Guy Owens Poetry Prize, the Georgia Writers Association Award, the *New England Review/Bread Loaf Quarterly* Narrative Poem Award, and a DeWitt Wallace/*Reader's Digest* Fellowship. He was the subject of a 1995 PBS documentary on poetry, "The Language of Life," hosted by Bill Moyers.

Roy Alton Blount Jr. (1941–   ) attended Vanderbilt University (B.A. magna cum laude 1963) and Harvard University (M.A. 1964). He has written for a number of newspapers and magazines, including *Sports Illustrated, Playboy, Rolling Stone, The New Yorker, Esquire,* and *The Atlantic Monthly. Crackers,* his collection of essays about the South and the Carter Administration (1980), brought him national attention and is his most consistently humorous work. Other books include *About Three Bricks Shy of a Load* (1974), *One Fell Soup, or, I'm Just a Bug on the Windshield of Life* (1982), *What Men Don't Tell Women* (1984), *Not Exactly What I Had in Mind* (1985), *Soupsongs: Webster's Ark* (1987), *Now Where Were We?* (1988), *First Hubby* (1990), *Camels Are Easy, Comedy's Hard* (1992), and *Be Sweet: A Conditional Love Story* (1998). He has also edited *Roy Blount's Book of Southern Humor* (1994).

Adrienne Bond (1933–1995) was a native of Montezuma, Georgia, and for many years a member of the English Department faculty at Mercer University. Her poems were published in such journals as *The Georgia Review, The New Yorker,* and *The Southern Review.* Her books include *Eugene W. Stetson* (1983), *The Voice of the Poet: The Shape and Sound of Southern Poetry Today* (1989), and *Time Was, She Declares: Selected Poems of Adrienne Bond* (1996).

David Bottoms (1949–   ) achieved wide recognition early in his career when Robert Penn Warren chose *Shooting Rats at the Bibb County Dump* (1979) for the Academy of American Poets Walt Whitman Award. Since then he has continued to write poetry and has also published two novels, *Any Cold Jordan* (1987) and *Easter Weekend* (1990). Bottoms holds a Ph.D. from Florida State University and is a professor of English at Georgia State University. His poetry collections include *In a U-Haul North of Damascus* (1982), *Under the Vulture-Tree* (1987), and *Armored Hearts: New and Selected Poetry* (1995). He has also co-edited, with Dave Smith, *The Morrow Anthology of Younger American Poets* (1985). Bottoms received the Book of the Year Award from the Dixie Council of Authors and Journalists, the Levinson Award from *Poetry* magazine, an Ingram-Merrill Award, and an Award in Literature from the American Academy and Institute of Arts and Letters.

Edgar Bowers (1924–) was born in Rome, Georgia, and educated at the University of North Carolina, where he received his B.A., and Stanford University, where he received his M.A. and Ph.D. He has taught at Duke University, Harper College, and the University of California at Santa Barbara, where he spent most of his academic career. His books include *The Form of Loss* (1964), *The Astronomers* (1965), *Living Together: New and Selected Poems* (1973), *Witnesses* (1981), *For Louis Pasteur* (1989), and *Collected Poems* (1997). He has held Fulbright and Guggenheim fellowships and has been the recipient of an Ingram-Merrill Award, a University of California Creative Arts Institute grant, and a Brandeis University creative arts award.

Van K. Brock (1932–) was born in Boston, Georgia. He received a B.A. from Emory University and M.A., M.F.A., and Ph.D. degrees from the University of Iowa. He has taught at numerous colleges and universities and for a number of years was a professor of English and director of the writing programs at Florida State University. His books of poetry include *Final Belief* (1972), *Spelunking* (1977), *Weighing the Penalties* (1978), *The Hard Essential Landscape* (1980), and *The Window* (1981). He has also edited several volumes of poetry by children and by inmates of the Florida penal system. He has received awards from the Kansas City Poetry Contest, the Georgia Writers' Association, and the Florida Poetry Contest and has held a Rockefeller fellowship.

Kathryn Stripling Byer (1944–) is a native of Camilla, Georgia. She holds a B.A. from Wesleyan College in Macon and a B.F.A. from the University of North Carolina at Greensboro, where she studied under Allen Tate and Fred Chappell. Her volumes of poetry include *Search Party* (1979), *Alma* (1983), *The Girl in the Midst of the Harvest* (1986), *Wildwood Flower* (1992, winner of the 1992 Lamont Selection by the American Academy of Poets), and *Black Shawl* (1998). She is a Fellow of the National Endowment for the Arts and a winner of the Anne Sexton Poetry Award and the Thomas Wolfe Literary Award. She is a professor of English at Western Carolina University, where she has taught since 1966.

Turner Cassity (1929–) was born in Jackson, Mississippi. He was educated at Millsaps College, Stanford University, and Columbia University. From 1962 to 1994 he was chief of the serials and binding department in the Emory University

Library. He is a prolific poet whose books include *Watchboy, What of the Night?* (1966), *Steeplejacks in Babel* (1973), *Silver out of Shanghai* (1973), *Yellow for Peril, Black for Beautiful* (1975), *The Defense of the Sugar Islands* (1979), *Keys to Mayerling* (1983), *The Airship Boys in Africa* (1984), *The Book of Alna* (1985), *Hurricane Lamp* (1986), *Between the Chains* (1991), and *The Destructive Element: New and Selected Poems* (1998). He has received the Blumenthal-Leviton-Blonder prize for poetry.

Pearl Cleage (1948–) is primarily known as a dramatist. Her work has been performed in Atlanta, New York, and Chicago. Among her plays are *puppetplay, Good News, Porch Songs, Banana Bread, Essentials,* and *Hospice.* Her published work includes *One for the Brothers* (short fiction, 1983), *We Don't Need No Music* (poetry, 1971), *The Brass Bed and Other Stories* (fiction and poetry, 1991), *Deals with the Devil and Other Reasons to Riot* (essays, 1993), *Flyin' West* (drama, 1995), and *What Looks Like Crazy on an Ordinary Day* (novel, 1997).

Judith Ortiz Cofer (1952–) is a native of Puerto Rico who moved to Paterson, New Jersey, with her family when she was four and to Augusta, Georgia, when she was fifteen. She holds a B.A. from Augusta College and an M.A. from Florida Atlantic University. Cofer works as a poet, novelist, and essayist, and she has been widely published and anthologized. Her books include *Peregrina* (poetry, 1986), *Terms of Survival* (poetry, 1987), *The Line of the Sun* (novel, 1989), *Silent Dancing* (essays and poems, 1990), *The Latin Deli* (essays and poems, 1993), and *An Island like You: Stories of the Barrio* (1995). Cofer is the recipient of the O. Henry Prize for Short Fiction, the Anisfield-Wolf Book Award, the Pushcart Prize, and many other awards and grants. She is a professor of English at the University of Georgia, where she has taught since 1992.

Stephen Corey (1948–) was born in Buffalo, New York, and educated at SUNY Binghamton, where he received his B.A., and the University of Florida, where he received his Ph.D. After teaching at the University of Florida and the University of South Carolina, he became assistant editor of *The Georgia Review* in 1981; he has been associate editor since 1985. His books of poetry include *Synchronized Swimming* (1985) and *All These Lands You Call One Country* (1992), for which he won the Georgia Writer of the Year Award. With Stanley Lindberg he has edited *Necessary Fictions: Selected Stories from the Georgia Review* (1986) and *Keener Sounds: Selected Poems from the Georgia Review* (1987).

Alfred Corn (1943–   ) is one of the most prolific and distinguished of Georgia poets. He was born in Bainbridge, Georgia, and attended Emory University, where he graduated with a B.A. in 1965. He earned his M.A. from Columbia University. He has worked as a freelance writer and editor and has taught at various colleges and universities. Currently he is an adjunct professor in the School of Arts at Columbia University. His collections of poetry include *All Roads at Once* (1976), *A Call in the Midst of the Crowd* (1978), *The Various Light* (1980), *Notes from a Child of Paradise* (1984), *The West Door* (1988), *Autobiographies: Poems* (1992), *The Pith Helmet: Aphorisms* (1992), and *Present* (1997). He has also published two critical books, *The Metamorphoses of Metaphor: Essays in Poetry and Fiction* (1987) and *Incarnation: Contemporary Writers on the New Testament* (1990), which he edited. He has received an Ingram-Merrill Award, the George Dillon Prize from *Poetry,* and the Blumenthal Prize.

Rosemary Daniell (1935–   ) was born and raised in Atlanta. A high school dropout at sixteen, she prepared for a career as a mother and housewife but discovered her passion for writing in a poetry workshop with James Dickey at Emory University. Her books include *A Sexual Tour of the Deep South* (poems, 1975), *Fatal Flowers: On Sin, Sex, and Suicide in the Deep South* (memoir, 1980), *Sleeping with Soldiers: In Search of the Macho Man* (memoir, 1985), *Fort Bragg and Other Points South* (poetry, 1988), *The Hurricane Season* (novel, 1992), and *The Woman Who Spilled Words All Over Herself* (memoir and self-help, 1997).

James Dickey (1923–1997) was born in Atlanta and graduated from North Fulton High School. After a year at Clemson University, he became a navigator, flew eighty-seven missions in the Pacific during World War II, and was awarded a Silver Star and two Distinguished Flying Crosses for valor. He graduated from Vanderbilt University magna cum laude in 1948 and earned his M.A. there in 1950. He held teaching positions at Rice University and the University of Florida, served in the U.S. Air Force during the Korean War, and worked as an advertising writer in New York and Atlanta. During the 1950s Dickey began writing poetry intensively. His first book of poems, *Into the Stone,* appeared in 1960; his second, *Drowning with Others,* in 1962. He received a Guggenheim fellowship in 1961, traveled in Europe, and taught at several American colleges. *Buckdancer's Choice* won the National Book Award for poetry in 1966 and *Poems: 1957–1967* secured his reputation as a major poet. Other volumes of poetry include *Helmets* (1964), *The Eye-Beaters, Blood, Victory, Madness, Buckhead and Mercy* (1970), *The Zo-*

diac (1976), *The Strength of Fields* (1979), *Puella* (1982), *The Eagle's Mile* (1990), and *Striking In: The Early Notebooks of James Dickey* (ed. Gordon Van Ness, 1996). His 1970 novel *Deliverance* was a best-seller and was made into a movie, for which he wrote the screenplay and in which he played a small role as a sheriff. Other novels include *Alnilam* (1988) and *To the White Sea* (1994). Dickey has also published four collections of highly original criticism. At the time of his death he was living in Columbia, South Carolina, where he was poet-in-residence at the University of South Carolina.

William Edward Burghardt (W. E. B.) Du Bois (1868–1963) was one of the most important and influential African American leaders of the twentieth century. He earned a Ph.D. from Harvard in 1896 and soon thereafter began to write and campaign on behalf of African Americans. His career traces a path from conservative moderation, like that of Booker T. Washington, to increasing activism, and finally to radicalism. He co-founded the NAACP in 1909 and as a leader and writer in that organization campaigned vigorously against segregation and racism. Eventually he found the NAACP too conservative and began to advocate segregation and Pan-Africanism. In the latter decades of his life his influence gradually waned. In 1961 he joined the communist party and in 1962 he became a citizen of Ghana, where he died a year later. Du Bois served on the faculty of Atlanta University from 1897 to 1910 and 1934 to 1944. He founded two important journals: *Crisis,* a publication of the NAACP, and *Phylon.* Among his important and influential writings are *The Souls of Black Folk* (1903), *Black Reconstruction in the South* (1935), and *Dusk of Dawn* (1940), an autobiography.

William Greenway (1947–) is a native of Atlanta. He received his B.A. from Georgia State University and his Ph.D. in modern literature and poetry from Tulane University. He is the author of *Pressure under Grace* (1982), *Where We've Been* (1987), *Father Dreams* (winner of the State Street Press Chapbook Competition, 1993), and *How the Dead Bury the Dead* (1994), for which he won the Georgia Author of the Year Award. He holds Distinguished Professorships in both Teaching and Scholarship at Youngstown State University, where he is a professor of English.

Walter Griffin (1937–) was born in Wilmington, Delaware, and educated at Ohio State University, where he received his B.A. He founded and became director of the Atlanta Poets Workshop. He was named Master-Poet-in-Residence for the Georgia Council for the Arts and Humanities in 1978 and from 1972 to 1983 served as a visiting writer in residence at 110 schools, colleges, and penal institutions in the state. He was named Georgia Poet of the Year in 1974 by the Dixie Council of Authors and Journalists for his collection *Other Cities*. His other books include *Leaving for New York* (1968), *Ice Garden* (1973), *Machineworks* (1976), *Poet Authority* (1976), *Skull Dreamer* (1977), and *Western Flyers*, the 1990 winner of the University of West Florida's Panhandler Series.

Georgia Douglas Johnson (1886–1966) was born in Atlanta. She studied at Oberlin College and Atlanta University and, after marrying a civil servant, moved to Washington, D.C., where she held various government jobs. Johnson was a significant figure in the Harlem Renaissance, a prominent historical dramatist, and one of the earliest African American women poets of the twentieth century. Her books include *The Heart of a Woman and Other Poems* (1918), *Bronze: A Book in Verse* (1922), *An Autumn Love Cycle* (1938), and *Share My World* (1962). Her poems are diverse in style and form, and they explore a wide range of themes. Sometimes regarded as a conservative poet whose use of traditional forms was at odds with the literary modernism of her day, she nonetheless wrote some of her strongest poems about African American and feminist themes.

Greg Johnson (1953–) is a poet, writer, and scholar who lives in Atlanta. A native of San Francisco, he earned his B.A. and M.A. at Southern Methodist University and his Ph.D. at Emory University. He is the author of *Emily Dickinson: Perception and the Poet's Quest* (1985), *Understanding Joyce Carol Oates* (1987), *Distant Friends* (stories, 1990), *A Friendly Deceit* (stories, 1992), *Pagan Babies* (novel, 1992), *Aid and Comfort* (poems, 1993), *Joyce Carol Oates: A Study of the Short Fiction* (1994), *I Am Dangerous* (stories, 1996), and *Invisible Writer: A Biography of Joyce Carol Oates* (1998). He received the O. Henry Award for short fiction in 1996 and was named Georgia Author of the Year in 1991. Since 1989 he has taught in the English Department at Kennesaw State University.

Sidney Lanier (1842–1881) was born into a cultured family in Macon and showed an early interest in music. He attended Oglethorpe University, graduated in 1860, and enlisted in the Confederate Army in 1861. Made a prisoner of war in 1864, by the time of his release he had contracted tuberculosis, which eventually caused his death. His novel *Tiger-Lilies*, written in three weeks, was published in 1867 and is based in part on his Civil War experiences. He married Mary Day of Macon in the same year; they became the parents of four sons, all raised in the poverty to which a poet-musician's income destined them. Lanier moved to Baltimore in 1873 and, when his health permitted, played the flute in an orchestra there. He composed most of his important poems during the last three years of his life. In 1879 he became a lecturer in English at Johns Hopkins University. Lanier is noted not only for his poetry but also for his theories on the relationship of music and poetry. He was one of the major American poets of the nineteenth century.

Frank Manley (1930–) was born in Cranton, Pennsylvania. He received his B.A. from Emory University and his M.A. and Ph.D. from Johns Hopkins University. He has taught at Emory University since 1964, where he is a professor of English. Publications include *Resultances* (poems, 1980), *Within the Ribbons* (short fiction, 1989), and *The Cockfighter* (novel, 1996), and he is coauthor with Floyd Watkins of *Some Poems and Some Talk about Poetry* (1985). He is the author of several plays produced at Emory University and by the Alliance Theater in Atlanta, and most recently his play *The Trap* was named by *Atlanta Magazine* as the Best New Play of 1994. He has also edited volumes of poetry by George Chapman and John Donne.

Frances Mayes (1940–) is a native of Americus, Georgia. She received her B.A. from the University of Florida and her M.A. from San Francisco State University, where she currently works as head of the Creative Writing Program. Her books include *Sunday in Another Country* (1977), *After Such Pleasures* (1979), *The Arts of Fire* (1981), *Hours* (1984), *The Discovery of Poetry* (1986), *Ex Voto* (1995), and *Under the Tuscan Sun: At Home in Italy* (1996). Her essays and poetry have appeared in *The Atlantic, The Virginia Quarterly Review, The American Scholar, The Southern Review, Manoa,* and *New American Writing.* She has received an award from the Academy of American Poets and the NEA Award in Poetry.

Susie Mee (1937–) grew up in Trion, Georgia, and after graduating from the University of Georgia attended Yale Drama School. During the 1960s and 1970s she was a professional actress in New York productions both on and off Broadway. In the 1980s she began to write, and her poetry first appeared in *The Georgia Review, Poetry, The Chicago Tribune, Sumac, Stand,* and *Perspective.* Her first collection of poems, *The Undertaker's Daughter,* appeared in 1992, and her novel, *The Girl Who Loved Elvis,* was published in 1993. She has also edited *Downhome: An Anthology of Southern Women Writers* (1995). She currently teaches creative writing at New York University.

Judson Mitcham (1948–) was born in Monroe, Georgia. He received his A.B., M.A., and Ph.D. degrees in psychology from the University of Georgia. He has taught at Fort Valley State College since 1974, where he serves as head of the Psychology Department. Mitcham's collection of poetry *Somewhere in Ecclesiastes* (1991) earned him the Devins Award from the University of Missouri Press and the Georgia Author of the Year Award in 1991 from the Council of Authors and Journalists. His novel *Sweet Everlasting* appeared in 1996. Mitcham's work has been published in *The Georgia Review, Gettysburg Review, The Southern Review, Southern Poetry Review, Poetry,* and numerous other prominent journals. He is an adjunct member of the creative writing faculties at Emory University and the University of Georgia.

Marion Montgomery (1925–) was born in Thomaston, Georgia. Montgomery studied in the University of Iowa writing program and earned B.A. and M.A. degrees in English from the University of Georgia. He became an instructor at the university in 1954, where he taught creative writing, lyric poetry, and modern literature until his retirement as a full professor in 1989. Montgomery's life has been that of a writer and scholar. He has published three novels, two volumes of poetry, and numerous essays and volumes of criticism, including a massive three-volume study of his friend Flannery O'Connor and of western culture in general entitled *The Prophetic Poet and the Popular Spirit.* Making full use of Southern tradition, folklore, and idiom, Montgomery's work offers a fierce indictment of what he regards as a corrupt and secularized modern world.

Eric Nelson (1952–) teaches in the Department of English and Philosophy at Georgia Southern University in Statesboro, Georgia. He was born in San Angelo, Texas, and as the child of an Air Force officer spent his childhood in such locations as Texas, Japan, Alabama, Ohio, and Virginia. He earned a B.A. from Virginia Technical Institute and an M.A. from the Johns Hopkins Writing Seminar in 1977. His books include *On Call* (1983), *The Light Bringers* (1984), and *Interpretation of Waking Life* (1991), which won the 1990 Arkansas Poetry Award.

Wyatt Prunty (1947–) was born in Humbolt, Tennessee, and grew up in Athens, Georgia. He received his B.A. from the University of the South, his M.A. from Johns Hopkins, and his Ph.D. from Louisiana State University. His books include *To My Father* (1982), *The Times Between* (1982), *What Women Know, What Men Believe* (1986), *Balance as Belief* (1989), *The Run of the House* (1993), and *Since the Noon Mail Stopped* (1997). He is also author of a critical study, *"Fallen from the symboled world": Precedents for the New Formalism* (1990). His work has been widely published in such places as *The New Yorker, New Republic, American Scholar, Kenyon Review, The Southern Review,* and *Sewanee Review.* He is Carlton Professor of English at the University of the South.

Byron Herbert Reece (1917–1958) grew up in the north Georgia mountains outside Dahlonega. He began writing at an early age, and his high school teachers were among the first to recognize his talent. He enrolled at Young Harris in 1935, dropped out, and reenrolled in 1938, writing poetry all the while. His poems caught the eye of *Atlanta Constitution* editor Ralph McGill, who met him while on a visit to Young Harris. Reece left college without graduating in 1940 and returned to his parents' farm to work. His poetry attracted the attention of Kentucky writer Jesse Stuart, who helped convince E. P. Dutton to publish Reece's first volume of poems, *Ballad of the Bones,* in 1945. Other volumes of poetry followed: *Remembrance of Moab* (1949), *Bow Down in Jericho* (1950), *A Song of Joy* (1952), and *The Season of Flesh* (1955). Reece received two Guggenheim fellowships in creative writing, served as poet-in-residence at UCLA in 1950, and spent a brief summer in an artist's colony in California. He committed suicide in 1958, apparently in despair over progressing tuberculosis. His novels *Better a Dinner of Herbs* (1950) and *The Hawk and the Sun* (1955) are unrecognized literary gems.

Alane Rollings (1950–   ) has published three books of poetry: *Transparent Landscapes* (1984), *In Your Sweet Time* (1989), and *In the Struggle to Adore* (1994). Her first book was a Writer's Choice Pushcart/NEA Selection for 1985. Born in Savannah, Georgia, she studied at Bryn Mawr and received her B.A. from the University of Chicago, where she also earned an M.A. in Far Eastern Languages and Civilizations. She is married to the novelist Richard Stern.

Larry Rubin (1930–   ) is a native of Bayonne, New Jersey. After a year at Columbia University, he enrolled at Emory University, where he earned his B.A., M.A., and Ph.D. degrees. He has been a faculty member in English at the Georgia Institute of Technology since 1956. His books include *The World's Old Way* (1962), *Lanced in Light* (1967), and *All My Mirrors Lie* (1975). He has received numerous awards for his work, including the Reynolds Lyric Award, the Georgia Writer's Association Literary Achievement Award, the Sidney Lanier Award, and the Poetry Society of America annual award. His poems have been widely published in well-known journals and anthologies.

Bettie Sellers (1926–) is well known as a poet of the North Georgia mountains. She was born in Tampa, Florida, and educated at LaGrange College, where she earned her B.A., and the University of Georgia, where she earned an M.A. She taught at Young Harris College from 1965 to 1995 and was appointed Chair of the Division of Humanities in 1975. Her books include *Westward from Bald Mountain* (1974), *Spring Onions and Cornbread* (1978), *Morning of the Red-tailed Hawk* (1981), *Liza's Monday and Other Poems* (1986), and *Wild Ginger* (1989). She has also published studies of Georgia writers Joel Chandler Harris and Byron Herbert Reece. She lives in Young Harris, Georgia. Her awards include the Author of the Year in Poetry (twice) from the Dixie Council of Authors and Journalists, Poet of the Year from the Southeastern Writers Association, the Caroline Wyatt Memorial Award, and the Daniel Whitehead Hickey Memorial National Award.

Charlie Smith (1947–) is the son of Georgia legislator Charles Smith Sr. and a native of Moultrie. Smith graduated from Duke University. He served two years in the Peace Corps, studied at the University of Iowa Writers Workshop, and edited the *Clayton Sun* newspaper before his story "Crystal River" was accepted by the *Paris Review* in 1977. It won the Aga Khan Prize for Fiction. Smith's first novel, *Canaan,* appeared in 1984. *Shine Hawk* followed in 1988, *The Lives of the Dead* in 1990, *Crystal River: Three Novellas* in 1991, and *Cheap Ticket to Heaven* in 1996. His collections of poetry include *Red Roads* (1987), *The Palms* (1993), and *Before and After* (1995). His work is marked by an intense lyricism, violence and eroticism, and psychological explorations into the contemporary human psyche. He lives in New York City.

Ron Smith (1949–) is a native of Savannah, Georgia. He attended the University of Richmond on a football scholarship and double-majored in philosophy and English. He earned an M.A. in English at the University of Richmond and his M.F.A. at Virginia Commonwealth University. He has received the 1986 Guy Owens Award for the title poem of his book *Running Again in Hollywood* (1988) as well as the Theodore Roethke Poetry Prize from *Poetry Northwest.* He has also served as poetry editor for the *Richmond Quarterly.* He has taught at Virginia Commonwealth University and at Mary Washington College and is currently writer-in-residence at the St. Christopher's School in Richmond, Virginia.

Leon Stokesbury (1945–) is a native of Arkansas who teaches in the creative writing program at Georgia State University. His two collections of poetry are *The Drifting Away* (1986) and *Autumn Rhythm: New and Selected Poems*

(1996). He has edited *The Made Thing: An Anthology of Contemporary Southern Poetry* (1987), *Articles of War: A Collection of American Poetry about World War II* (1990), and *The Light the Dead See: Selected Poems of Frank Stanford* (1991).

John Stone (1936–) has maintained a double career as a cardiologist and as a writer and poet. After earning his M.D. at Washington University in St. Louis in 1962, he did postdoctoral study at the University of Rochester and then at Emory University, whose staff he joined in 1969. His books include *The Smell of Matches* (1972, for which he won the Georgia Writers Association achievement award for poetry), *In All This Rain* (1980), *January: A Flight of Birds* (1983), *Renaming the Streets* (1985), and *In the Country of Hearts: Journeys in the Art of Medicine* (essays, 1990). He co-edited with Richard Reynolds *On Doctor(i)ng: stories, poems, essays* (1995).

Nathan Eugene (Jean) Toomer (1894–1967) was born in Washington, D.C. His maternal grandfather, the controversial P. B. S. Pinchback, was a Macon native who served as acting governor of Louisiana during Reconstruction. In his youth Toomer frequently changed schools, political persuasions, career plans, and religions. He spent only three months in Georgia, serving as temporary principal of an industrial and agricultural school for blacks in Sparta, but from that brief stay came the novel for which he is remembered. *Cane* was published in 1923 to general acclaim and is one of the most important works of the Harlem Renaissance. Later in his life Toomer became evasive about his racial identity, stopped writing about the black experience, and became an adherent of the spiritualist self-realization movement of George Gurdjieff. With the exception of one privately printed book, he published only occasional pieces after *Cane* and left at his death a large body of unpublished work.

Alice Walker (1944–) was born into a large sharecropping family in Eatonton, Georgia, and graduated first in her high school class. She attended Spellman College in Atlanta for two years before transferring to Sarah Lawrence College in New York. In Atlanta she was active in the civil rights movement, and at Sarah Lawrence she studied writing under Muriel Rukeyser. Her first book, a collection of poems, *Once,* appeared in 1968; her first novel, *The Third Life of Grange Copeland,* followed in 1970. Walker is especially skillful as a writer of short fiction, as her collection *In Love and Trouble: Stories of Black Women* (1973) demonstrates. Two stories from the volume ("Everyday Use" and "The Revenge of Hannah Kemhuff") appeared in *Best American Short Stories* for 1974. Her

1976 novel *Meridian* in part concerns the transformative effect of the civil rights movement on one of its participants. In the 1970s Walker served as an editor of *Ms.* magazine, and in 1977 she won a Guggenheim fellowship. *The Color Purple,* her widely acclaimed novel about an oppressed young black woman's gradual struggle toward self-discovery, appeared in 1982. It was a best-seller and won both the Pulitzer Prize and the American Book Award in 1982. A film based on the novel appeared in 1985. *Living by the Word: Selected Writings, 1973–1987* appeared in 1988, and another novel, *The Temple of My Familiar,* in 1989. Her collections of poetry include *Once* (1968), *Horses make a landscape look more beautiful* (1984), *Her Blue Body Everything We Know: Earthling Poems, 1965– 1990* (1991).

Philip Lee Williams (1950–   ) was born in Madison, Georgia, where he has lived for much of his life. After earning an A.B. in journalism from the University of Georgia in 1972, Williams spent much of the next fifteen years in newspaper work. He was associate editor of *The Madisonian* from 1974 to 1978 and editor of the *Athens Observer* from 1978 to 1985. He also wrote fiction throughout these years, at first for his own entertainment, then with ambitions to publish. In 1984 his first novel, *In the Heart of a Distant Forest* (the title comes from a line in James Dickey's poem "The Lifeguard"), was published by W. W. Norton. Other novels since then include *All the Western Stars* (1988), *Slow Dance in Autumn* (1988), *The Song of Daniel* (1989), *Perfect Timing* (1991), *Final Heat* (1992), *Blue Crystal* (1993), and *The True and Authentic History of Jenny Dorset* (1997). Two recent nonfiction books are *The Silent Stars Go By* (1998), a Christmas reminiscence, and *Crossing Wildcat Ridge: A Memoir of Nature and Healing* (1999), an account of the author's experience with open heart surgery. Williams has published poems in *Poetry* and has edited and published *Ataraxia,* a poetry journal.